money
forever

how to make your money
last as long as you do

money forever

Donald Ray Haas

foreword by **Murray Feldman**

Crofton Creek Press
South Boardman, Michigan

First Edition
10 9 8 7 6 5 4 3 2 1

Published by Crofton Creek Press
2303 Gregg Road SW
South Boardman, Michigan 49680
E-mail: croftoncreek@traverse.net
Web site: www.croftoncreek.com

Cover design by Angela Saxon, Saxon Design Inc., Traverse City, Michigan

The text of this book was set in Bembo, a typeface modeled on typefaces
cut by Francesco Griffo in 1495 for a book by classicist Pietro Bembo
(1470–1547). Griffo's design is considered one of the first of the old style
typefaces that were used as staple text types in Europe for 200 years.

Contents

Foreword

Orchestrating life's dreams takes planning, discipline, and years of learning. If you haven't mapped out a plan for stretching your *Money Forever*, you're now in luck. Donald Haas has done the hard work for you.

I was introduced to Don through a news release that crossed my desk during the bull market of the late 1980s. Unlike others who were promoting the roaring stock market as a lottery ticket that couldn't miss, Don was methodical. He spoke of the averages, not for the Dow Jones, the Standard & Poor's, or the NASDAQ, but for inflation, life expectancy, and real investment gains.

In retrospect, his message was sound, his mathematics simple. The averages tell us you're going to live to a certain age and that regardless of what the stock market does today, you can only expect a 10 percent annual return, and inflation will steal 3 percent of that. So, you'd better plan accordingly. That's what Don has been helping people do for over four decades.

His goal is to keep his clients financially fit until their last day on earth. That often prompts uneasy conversations. He's looked many a client in the eye and said, "Here's the date you'll probably die!" He then proceeds to tell them how much money they're going to have to find to make it worthwhile to see that age. Don goes to work examining every bill they pay, every cent that comes into their home, and every expense they're going to incur "forever."

When he presents the master plan, it also includes directions to follow to make sure the people you leave behind will be able to maximize what you won't be taking with you. We're talking estate planning!

Clients have called him "brutally honest," even "dramatic." Don is a bit of a showman, but that comes naturally. This maestro of money became a cornet player at the age of nine and was a member of the Detroit Symphony Orchestra for twenty years. He realizes that, like his music, the management of money takes strict discipline. He entered financial services to look for solutions to his own financial crises. As he began sharing his knowledge with others, he was helping craft what was to become the fastest growing field in America—financial planning. His efforts were rewarded when, in 2001, he was presented with the prestigious Loren Dunton Memorial Award for significant contributions to the financial advising profession and the public.

In the midst of the last bear market, I asked him if he was getting calls from panic-stricken clients. "A few," he replied, "but not many." "How's that?" I inquired. His response surprised me. "More than 90 percent of my clients are still increasing their net worth even with the market down 30 percent and more."

In early 2000, as the headlines screamed disaster with banners like "Market Crash" and "Wall Street Washout," Don was continuing to create millionaires!

In the following pages, you'll meet many of them. Here, they have names like Jan and John Justus, Daphne and Dudley Do-right, and two of my favorites, Jamie and Grandpa. But these people are really you and me at every stage of our lives. They have the questions, the fears, and the concerns that we all have, but they're getting the answers that we all need if we are to find *Money Forever*.

In order to benefit from the lessons in this book, you'll have to stay healthy. Don covers that, too, not only here but also in his practice. His clients receive a monthly financial letter, which also often contains updates on Don's most recent medical check-ups and general health. Don knows you need both wealth and health to be happy. He can rattle off how many pounds an adult should gain each year, along with how much their investments should grow. Clients are invited to his home to celebrate his special birthdays and a bi-annual Oktoberfest observance. He never forgets to drop a birthday card in the mail for his clients and their loved ones.

You are holding in your hand a master plan for financial fitness—the results of a lifetime of research and advice from a man who has been a loyal friend, a valuable news source, and a trusted advisor. Here's hoping you enjoy *Money Forever* . . . in more ways than one!

Murray Feldman
News Anchor/Money Editor
WJBK TV Fox 2
WWJ News Radio 950

Acknowledgments

Robert L. Spence, for sharing with me his forty years of experience in the publishing business, for acting as my personal editor on all aspects of the development of the manuscript for this book, and most important, for being a good friend.

Carol L. Edwards, for being my companion and best friend and for giving me both moral and physical support, not only in the writing of this book, but in all the activities in which I have participated during the past twenty-five years.

Mark Davis, for being my partner and friend and exploring with me the many technical and conceptual aspects of financial planning, and for suggesting the title of this book.

Susan Farmer, for sharing her expertise in communication through the written word.

introduction

A New Beginning

The twentieth century will be remembered for many accomplishments, not the least of which is the development of the concept of retirement. Actually, American Express created the first pension plan in 1875, but the significance of retirement was not fully appreciated until well into the twentieth century.

Now, as we find ourselves in the early years of the twenty-first century, we find that the concept of leaving a lifetime career at a certain age, date, or time of life—that is, *retirement*—is undergoing a major transformation. What was thought to be appropriate for the industrial age, whether it was or not, is being replaced with a much better concept for the new age, one that allows each person to choose that which best fits his or her own set of circumstances.

This new concept of retirement involves a more active, engaging, and productive way of life. It involves choices of shortened workweeks, temporary work, working from home, or no work at all. Since chronological age is no longer relevant, and the aging experience itself is different for each individual, the new retirement will be so unlike the old that the word *retirement* will cease to properly describe this period of life.

Retirement, or whatever you might want to call it, has become simply one of the many stages of life. This stage may be filled either by continuing a long-standing career, embarking on a new career in a new or related field, or giving up completely any notion of employment. It is a time of life that can be anything an individual desires.

For some, the choice to continue working will be ordained by the need to maintain an acceptable standard of living. This is the worst reason to continue working. Whether you work or not in later life should be based on desire, not need. Being forced to do something you do not like can lead to misery, even illness. This book will help you avoid finding yourself in such a position.

Of course, there are certain "musts" in life. You must eat and you must breathe. Each culture also places additional demands on its citizens, such as wearing clothes, obeying community laws and procedures, and waiting until a certain age before enjoying a privilege. Within such restrictions, however, each of us has many choices, including what we do for a living, where we live, who we share our life with, and so on.

The new century offers an impressive array of choices as we progress through life. During this progression, retirement should be whatever you choose for yourself. It should occur whenever it fits into your personal plans. If it involves an increase, cessation, or reduction in earned income, it should be because you planned for such a contingency.

What is important is that you create an all-inclusive life plan, allowing for all the choices. To have *Money Forever* you must develop the proper resources, investing not so much for retirement as for the future.

chapter 1

How Saving for the Future Has Changed Since Your Grandfather's Time

Let's pretend.

Go back in time to the year 1932. Your grandfather has just retired. Grandfather doesn't know it yet, but he will live thirty more years—an unusually long time back then—to the year 1961.

Let's explore Grandfather's mental attitudes at the time he retired. The years before 1932 made an indelible impression on Grandfather. For example, five of the six years from 1926 through 1931 were marked by deflation. As you know, deflation is the opposite of inflation. In other words, it is negative inflation.

Year	Inflation Rate
1926	-1.5%
1927	-2.1%
1928	-1.0%
1929	+0.2%
1930	-6.0%
1931	-9.5%

Grandfather also watched the stock market crash as the Dow Jones Industrial Average, the most widely watched barometer of the U.S. stock market, plummeted from 381 to 41, a nearly 90 percent free-fall to basement levels. The government discontinued the gold standard,[1] and Grandfather found himself living in the worst depression[2] in the nation's history.

In preparation for his retirement, Grandfather read the current textbooks on investing. They all taught that retirement money should be kept in a safe place. So Grandfather put all his assets in a shoebox and waited for things to settle. It was a good decision because in 1932 there was 10.3 percent deflation, and by the end of his first year of retirement, Grandfather had increased the purchasing power of his money over 10 percent. That meant that for every $1.00 in his shoebox, Grandfather could buy $1.10 in goods and services.

The next year, 1933, the inflation rate was one-half of one percent (0.5 percent), but Grandfather believed this was an aberration similar to 1929. So he didn't worry. But when inflation continued each year for five straight years through the mid-1930s, Grandfather began to question his shoebox decision.

Still being cautious, he moved some of his assets into long-term U. S. government bonds, considered by many people as the safest bonds in the world. Then just about the time Grandfather thought he should do something more daring, the country again experienced deflation, -2.8 percent in 1938 and -0.5 percent in 1939. What Grandfather could not foresee is that back-to-back years of deflation would never happen again in his lifetime. In fact, he would see only two more years of deflation, -1.8 percent in 1949 and -0.5 percent in 1954. Even so, his conclusion that safety was the most important investment strategy in retirement served him well.

Inflation began to heat up in the 1940s. Even before the attack on Pearl Harbor on December 7, 1941, and the beginning of World War II, the rate of inflation reached 9.7 percent. After World War II ended in 1946, the rate of inflation was 18.2 percent. That same year, Grandfather's government bonds lost 0.1 percent, which meant that he lost 18.3 percent of the purchasing power of his assets in one year. What he could buy for $1.00 in 1945 cost $1.18 by the end of 1946.

At this time, he was barely halfway through his retirement years. By 1954 the rate of inflation settled down a bit, and the average annual inflation rate for Grandfather's remaining years was 1.3 percent.

Grandfather's obituary mentioned, among other attributes and accomplishments, his knowledge of financial matters and his acute awareness of proper investing for and during retirement. Yes, Grandfather studied the textbooks, and he did well practicing their safety-first advice.

Annual Inflation 1932–1961

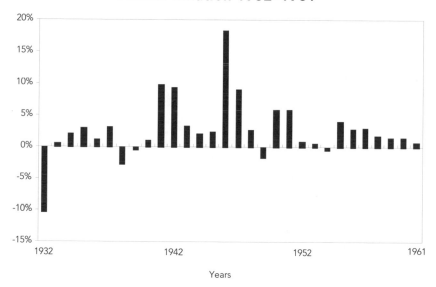

Years

Grandfather's son, your father, always respected his father's acumen in financial matters. So, when Father retired the year after Grandfather died, he looked forward to experiencing similar years of retirement. After all, Father had been the beneficiary of both Grandfather's wisdom and his financial textbooks, which Father proudly displayed on his bookshelves.

Father considered investing in long-term government bonds, as Grandfather had done so successfully. Father decided, however, that he also should make some adjustments in his investments to address the seemingly persistent problem of inflation. The rate

saving for the future

of inflation had averaged 1.7 percent during the seven years prior to Father's retirement. He worried about how long this inflation would continue and what kind of investments might help offset the erosive effects of inflation.

Now you and I know that inflation not only continued but reached double-digit rates in 1974 (12.2 percent), 1979 (13.3 percent), and 1980 (12.4 percent). Three shots like this hitting the value of anyone's assets could leave a poorly prepared person reeling from the blows, particularly when there were no years of deflation to offset some of the losses in purchasing power.

Annual Inflation 1962–1991

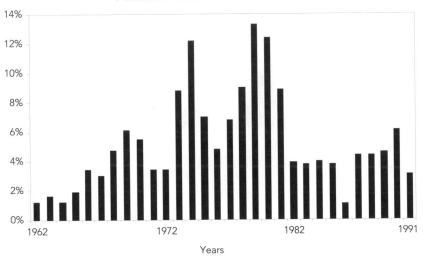

Years

Well, your father was not all that poorly prepared. Although he had a great concern about the risk of the stock market (learned from his father), he read newer books and articles. These materials helped him discover one way for a small investor to minimize the risks when investing in stocks: to invest in mutual funds, in which investors pool their investment money with other investors and have the benefit of professional investment advice.

Being cautious like his father, your father invested only a few hundred dollars in a stock mutual fund at the beginning of his retirement. By the end of the year, 1962, he had lost over 8 percent of this investment. Father was glad that he had invested only hundreds instead of thousands. But by the end of the following year, 1963, he witnessed the Standard & Poor's 500 Index (S&P 500), a broad-based barometer of the stock market, increase over 22 percent, causing him to wish he had invested thousands, not just hundreds, in the stock market.

Actually, you can be proud of your father. As a first-time investor in the stock market, he lived through an excellent learning experience. He lost money the first year, at least on paper, but he didn't sell. He hung on and was rewarded with a substantial gain on his original investment by the end of the second year of retirement.

Father began to invest more and more of his personal assets in stock mutual funds. He questioned the wisdom of this move when the stock market yielded a negative return, especially during the long bear market[3] of 1973 and 1974, when the S&P 500 had negative returns of -14.7 percent and -26.4 percent, respectively. Yet during the three decades Father invested in stocks, the investments produced more than enough growth to offset a very large amount of inflation.

Standard & Poor's 500
Annual Return 1962–1991

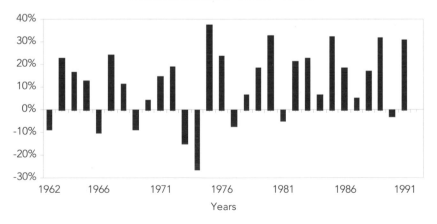

When Father died in 1991, he had been sufficiently successful to leave you a small legacy of investments and, of course,

Grandfather's financial textbooks augmented by some of his own.

Now it is your turn to prepare for retirement. You probably have many concerns about this. What kind of investments should be in your portfolio?[4] How much inflation might you experience in the future? How long will you live? How much income will you need, and where will it come from?

These questions and others will be addressed in the following chapters. All the topics are important, but if you have a special interest in a particular topic, feel free to go directly to that chapter. Don't postpone too long, however, the reading of Chapter 2, which deals with your life expectancy. How long you live will have an important effect on how you treat each of the other aspects of your journey into this new world of retirement.

notes

1. Gold Standard: a monetary standard under which the basic unit of currency is defined by a stated quantity of gold.

2. Depression: a period of low general economic activity marked especially by unemployment.

3. Bear Market: a period during which securities prices generally follow a downward trend. The term is used to describe either a historical period of price declines or an anticipated decline in prices. Its counterpart is a bull market, a period during which securities prices generally follow an upward trend.

4. Portfolio: an investment portfolio can consist of common stocks, bonds, money-market funds, mutual funds, commodities, options, precious metals, real estate, and so forth. Each portfolio should be custom-made to fit the needs of the individual investor.

chapter 2

Live Long . . . and Well

Just how long can one really expect to live? Had you lived in ancient Rome, only 40 percent of your neighbors would have lived to be twenty years old or older, and only 20 percent would have lived to be forty years old or older.

Compare that with a more recent time in the United States. In 1976, 80 percent of the people who were born sixty years earlier were still alive, and 40 percent of those born eighty years earlier also were still alive and kicking. Since 1976, there is more and more evidence to indicate that we are living even longer; much longer, in some cases.

Back in 1963, Clement G. Martin, M.D., wrote the book *How to Live to Be 100, Actively, Healthily, Vigorously*. In the introduction, he wrote: "In fact, one hundred and twenty-five years of activity and vitality should be the attainable goal of mankind. All other mammals live for five times the number of years it takes them to reach maturity. Man reaches his skeletal maturity about the age of twenty-six."

What Dr. Martin is saying is that if we lived as long as other mammals do, relative to skeletal maturity, our life expectancy would be five times twenty-six years, or 130 years. Dr. Martin also states, "Our job today [1963] is to take this average American life expectancy of 68 years and double it."

Roy L. Walford, M.D., professor of pathology at the UCLA School of Medicine, prepared a life-extension curve in 1976 to demonstrate his view of what the future holds regarding life expectancy. His view appeared in the July 1976 issue of *Fortune* magazine in the article "Science Is On the Trail of the Fountain of Youth."

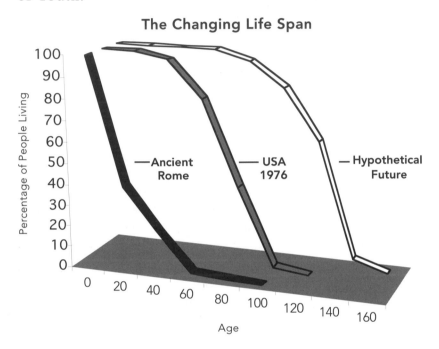

The Changing Life Span

Anticipating the influence of medical breakthroughs, Walford believed that the different stages of life will expand. In the future, rather than entering the aging-adult stage in your 60s, you will not enter this stage until age 100.

Since Walford created his curve of life expectancy in 1976, we have seen more evidence of people living not only longer but also healthier lives. As a result, more people marry at a later age and delay parenting until their 30s or early 40s. As shown in the diagram, life's traditional milestones are occurring later and later.

The Changing Life Milestones

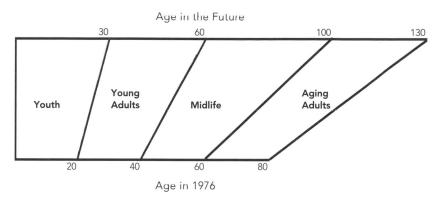

Age in the Future

| 30 | 60 | 100 | 130 |

Youth

Young Adults

Midlife

Aging Adults

| 20 | 40 | 60 | 80 |

Age in 1976

Some researchers believe that the human body could last for 160 years. Others believe that there may be no limit to the number of years that we could continue highly functional existences. Think about it. Here you are, 60 years old and thinking that retirement is just around the corner. Most of your life you thought you would be lucky if you reached 60 and then lived ten or twenty years more. Now you find out that you might live to be 100 years old. Don't you wish you could go back and do some things differently?

A wag once said, "If I had known I would live this long, I would have taken better care of myself." That saying is just as applicable to taking care of your wealth as to taking care of your health. Before we discuss how to maintain your financial wealth during all these extra years, here is additional information on how to maintain your physical health.

Regardless of how long you live, you want to be healthy so you can enjoy life. One way to maintain your health, as well as lengthen your life, is very simple: adopt the right mental attitude. The Book of Mark in the New Testament tells us, "If thou canst believe, all things are possible to him that believeth." Matthew gives us similar advice: "If ye have faith . . . nothing shall be impossible unto you . . . According to your faith, be it unto you." Believe that you will be healthy and will live a long life, and it may happen.

In more modern times, psychologist William James wrote, "Our belief at the beginning of a doubtful undertaking is the one thing that insures the successful outcome of your venture." If what we think comes from the control center of our body—the mind—then does it not make sense that we do and become what we think? In his books (combined in one volume) *The Will to Believe* and *Human Immortality*, James wrote, "Be not afraid of life. Believe that life is worth living, and your belief will help create the fact . . . Your faith beforehand in an uncertified result will make the result come true."

In *Age Wave: How the Most Important Trend of Our Time Will Change Our Future*, Ken Dychtwald, Ph.D., writes, "History has taught us that we tend to do and become what we expect to do and become. We fulfill our own prophecies." Think health, be healthy. Think young, be young.

Deepak Chopra, M.D., tells us in his books and classes that we can change our world, including our bodies, simply by changing our perception, or how we look at and interpret things. In *Ageless Body, Timeless Mind: The Quantum Alternative to Growing Old*, he writes, "The decline of vigor in old age is largely the result of people expecting to decline; they have unwittingly implanted a self-defeating intention in the form of a strong belief, and the mind–body connection automatically carries out this intention."

Does this mean that if we think we will die within a certain range of years, we will? Here again is what Dr. Chopra says: "Our fear of aging and our deep belief that we are meant to grow old may get transformed into aging itself, as a self-fulfilling prophecy generated by a withering self-image." Maybe the brain does start to shut down operations at a certain time programmed by all the things we have heard and read and implanted into our minds.

Reality is only what we perceive it to be. If we are brainwashed into believing that we will die according to certain mortality tables, then perhaps this is what we will do. Perhaps back in ancient Rome, people expected to die by age 35, and so most of them did. Of course, many of them died because their society did not have the medical knowledge and techniques available today, but even today's rapid advances in medicine and genetic science will be of no value to a person with a negative attitude.

What do you suppose might happen if we took advantage of modern medical knowledge and treatment and combined it with a firm belief that we shall live for a very long time? With mind and body working together, many of us might easily make it over the age-100 hurdle.

In his book *Dare to Be 100*, Walter M. Bortz II, M.D., writes, "A journey of a hundred miles or years begins, not with the first movement forward, but with the thought that precedes it . . . How you, like the turtle, set your course is highly predictive of the journey you will take."

In the March–April 1994 issue of *The Futurist,* Marvin Cetron published an article titled "An American Renaissance in the Year 2000: 74 Trends That Will Affect America's Future—and Yours." Cetron writes, "By 2005, look for a breakthrough in aging research to provide 115 to 120 years of vigorous good health."

Want more evidence? Consider what Raymond Daynes, an immunologist at the University of Utah, says: "I believe that over the next few years we are going to prove beyond a shadow of a doubt that some of the physiological changes which are used to define old age are totally preventable." James Vaupel of the Max Planck Institute for Demographic Research in Germany says, "There is no end in sight to the ever-increasing human life span. I think the debate is over. What's now emerging is a new paradigm of aging."

Since there is mounting evidence indicating longer and longer life expectancies, let us assume that the only prudent financial plan is one that extends to at least age 100. Of course, if at 90 things are going well for you, then it would be prudent to alter this time horizon and recalculate the need for income beyond the age of 100. Younger baby boomers should be developing methods for maintaining their health and wealth for a life expectancy of 120 years.

Of course, even if you have super genes, it still is incumbent on you to take care of yourself. Longevity seems to be based as much or more on lifestyle as on genes. The famous Danish Twin Study conducted between 1870 and 1888, with the data still being used in research today, shows that only 30 percent of longevity is due to genetic factors. Dr. Bortz concludes, "In other words, it's not the cards you're dealt that matter most, it's how you play your hand."

Dr. Fred Stransky, director of the Meadow Brook Health Enhancement Institute at Oakland University in Rochester, Michigan, believes that the ratio of the effects of lifestyle to the effects of genes could be as much as 9 to 1. In other words, 90 percent of your physical well-being is based on your lifestyle and only 10 percent on your genes. Dr. Stransky acknowledges that most people have difficulty in accepting this high ratio in favor of lifestyle because they don't understand the extensive power of lifestyle decisions. However, those people who choose to optimize their life through proper lifestyle decisions are benefited with a quality of functionality otherwise unobtainable.

In their book, *Living to 100: Lessons in Living to Your Maximum Potential at Any Age*, Drs. Thomas T. Perls and Margery Hutter Silver take an extended view that adds more perspective on the issue. "People who live to their seventies, eighties, and nineties in good health can make up for less protective genes by forming good health habits and by avoiding unnecessary hurdles, like smoking, excessive alcohol use, and sun exposure. But people who live to 100, particularly men, must have an extremely strong set of genes that protect them from damage from internal and external sources, such as free radicals and environmental hazards."

Drs. Perls and Silver further state, "The average person is born with strong enough longevity genes to live to age 85 and maybe longer. People who take appropriate preventive steps may add as many as ten quality years to that."

If anything like this information is correct, then you should appreciate this brief journey into the nonfinancial area of your life. Wealth without health should not be an acceptable alternative for you.

Regardless of your opinion on longevity, you will be well served if you take the proper amount of time to consider the following two proposals. First, your future years will be enhanced financially by letting the dust accumulate on Grandfather's old textbooks, which prescribed safety above all. Second, unless you currently have a significant and serious medical problem, prepare yourself for a very long period of retirement.

Just as wealth without health should not be an acceptable equation to you, neither should health without wealth. Read on to learn how to make your money last as long as you do.

chapter 3

Inflation—The Insidious Threat to a Prosperous Retirement

The word *insidious* describes that which spreads harmfully in a subtle or stealthy manner. It certainly is an appropriate adjective to describe *inflation*.

Inflation is a technical term that even experts have difficulty understanding. But don't you worry; what I have to say about inflation will be both basic and understandable . . . and all you really need to know. Just recognize that inflation affects us in devastating ways, and we each must find ways to cope.

Inflation is an economic condition characterized by a sustained rise in most prices. Here is how it is affecting you right now. You think you have a good income, but it doesn't seem to go as far anymore. You wonder what you are doing wrong. The answer is, you are doing nothing wrong. You are being affected by one of the outcomes of inflation. Sight unseen, inflation decreases the purchasing power of your money. You are right when you think your money doesn't go as far anymore. It doesn't.

Inflation doesn't just mean rising prices. Its effects are more far-reaching. For some people, particularly those on fixed incomes like many retirees are, it can mean a diminishing standard of living from which there might be no recovery.

So, how can you escape the effects of inflation? First, so we can better understand this monster, let's look at a little history.

Then we'll consider the future and how we can affect it to our benefit.

Look at the graph below for the ten-year span between 1930 and 1939. During this period, one-half of the years were deflationary; that is, the effect on our purchasing power was the opposite to that of inflation. Our dollars bought *more* goods and services. By the end of 1932, for example, a dollar bought 10 percent more than it did at the beginning of that year. Another way to put this is to say that a dollar you had on January 1, 1932, was worth $1.10 on December 31, 1932. There has not been another decade to match the 1930s. In fact, since that decade, there have been only two years of deflation, 1949 and 1954. All the other years were inflationary.

Annual Inflation/Deflation Rates
1926–2001

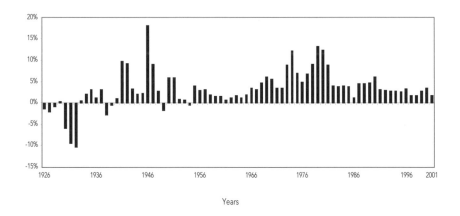

Years

Consider the seventy-six-year period from 1926 through 2001. The average rate of inflation for this period was 3.1 percent. This means that, for all practical purposes, any money you had in 1926 was worth 3.1 percent less each and every year thereafter. Remember that we are talking about an *average*. In 1946, a dollar would buy about 18 percent *less* than it did in 1945. When we consider investing assets for retirement, it is the average rate of inflation that concerns us. It makes sense to work with averages because no person can consistently predict each annual rate of inflation or each annual rate of return on investments.

Now, let's put all this in perspective. Keep in mind that we have had inflation every year but two from 1940 up to and including 2001, and we have had inflation *every* year from 1955 through 2001. We have had inflation in the past, we have inflation now, and in all probability, we will have inflation in the future. Unlike the common cold, which may seem to last forever but finally does go away, inflation just keeps hanging around.

Average Rate of Inflation

Years	Dates	Average Rate of Inflation
70	1932–2001	3.6%
60	1942–2001	4.1%
50	1952–2001	3.9%
40	1962–2001	4.5%
30	1972–2001	5.0%
20	1982–2001	3.6%
10	1992–2001	2.5%

Almost everyone is hurt by inflation, but retirees are hurt the most. While employed, a worker's earned income often is increased as inflation increases. The employer can give an employee this increase because inflation also provides an excuse to raise the price of the employer's product or service. Retirees, however, are often on fixed incomes.[1]

In most cases, a retiree's income is from three sources: Social Security, employer retirement plans, and personal assets. Social Security currently is adjusted annually for inflation, although each year the government addresses this proviso and considers its reduction or elimination. The automatic increase is costly and therefore is a tempting place for Congress to make cuts when seeking a future balance of income and outgo for our Social Security system. Except as a letter writer, a voter, or a political contributor, the retiree has no control over any of this. Most employer retirement plans have zero adjustments for inflation. The retiree has no control over these plans either. The retiree's investment portfolio is about the only place where the retiree has some control over the effects of inflation.

Historically, the investment portfolios of personal assets for retirees have been heavily weighted in fixed-dollar-type vehicles, such as certificates of deposit (CDs), Treasury bills, and bonds. In many cases, 100 percent of these assets were in "safe" savings accounts. Although many savings accounts are insured against loss up to a certain limit, these accounts provide virtually no protection against the effects of inflation.[2]

Now, is it any wonder why so many retirees are vulnerable to inflation when only one out of the three parts of their incomes is significantly adjusted for inflation? And that part—Social Security—is challenged annually by the government.

By now you should recognize that inflation is insidious and devastating, and if you plan and expect to have an increasing life expectancy, you must give proper attention to the effect inflation has on your assets. Such attention now and forever is important for your financial health.

So, how do you cope with inflation? You probably have already taken the first step, and that is to recognize that, in all probability, there will be future inflation. One of my clients described it as follows.

Although you must take this essential first step, you must do more than acknowledge the presence and effects of inflation. As you plan your income stream over all of your retirement years, it is imperative that you provide for an increase in future income on an annual basis. (See Chapter 6 for details on how to accomplish this.)

The next step is to adopt an investment portfolio that predominantly includes growth-type investments. (See Chapter 12 for details.)

Finally, be very careful not to be persuaded by those who challenge the validity of using the Consumer Price Index (CPI) as a proper indicator of inflation. The CPI is a measure of the average change in the prices paid by consumers for a "fixed" market basket of goods and services. Now some of you will say, "Hey, just what's in that market basket? I know that I pay more for gasoline than those folks in oil-producing states or in states with no or low taxes on fuel." Others of you might say, "Yo, I'm a city dweller. My food bills have to be higher than those for people living in rural areas or on farms." You farm folks might respond, "Yeah, but you guys have all the discount outlets. We have to pay more for clothing and appliances than you folks do."

The CPI is an average. It does not represent the exact prices for specific items in a specific place. It may not even represent the exact prices for specific items in any place. The CPI does represent, as best as possible, everyplace in general.

Components of the CPI

Year	Food	Clothing	Housing	Transpor-tation	Health Care	Entertain-ment	Composite
1981	7.8	4.8	11.5	12.2	10.7	7.8	8.9
1982	4.1	2.6	7.2	4.1	11.6	6.6	3.9
1983	2.1	2.5	2.7	2.4	8.8	4.3	3.8
1984	3.8	1.9	4.1	4.4	6.2	3.7	4.0
1985	2.3	2.8	4.0	2.6	6.3	4.0	3.8
1986	3.2	0.9	3.0	-3.9	7.5	3.4	1.1
1987	4.1	4.4	3.0	3.0	6.6	3.3	4.4
1988	4.1	4.3	3.8	3.1	6.5	4.3	4.4
1989	5.8	2.8	3.8	5.0	7.7	5.2	4.6
1990	5.8	4.6	4.5	5.6	9.0	4.7	6.1
1991	3.6	3.7	4.0	2.7	8.7	4.5	3.1
1992	1.6	1.4	2.6	3.0	6.6	2.8	2.9
1993	2.7	0.5	2.6	1.9	5.1	2.9	2.7
1994	2.5	-0.8	2.4	4.3	4.9	2.4	2.7
1995	2.4	0.5	2.9	1.9	4.0	3.2	2.5
1996	3.6	-0.3	3.0	3.6	2.9	2.7	3.3
1997	2.2	0.2	2.1	1.6	2.7	1.5	1.7
1998	2.3	-1.5	2.2	-1.6	3.6	1.4	1.6
1999	1.5	-0.9	2.5	5.6	3.6	0.6	2.7
2000	2.3	-1.3	3.5	6.2	4.1	1.3	3.4
20-Year Average	3.4%	1.7%	3.8%	3.4%	6.4%	3.5%	3.6%

The data in the chart show the annual rate of inflation for each component of the CPI. This information may help you determine how much you currently differ from the norm, or might differ in the future as your usage of the components changes. In retirement, for example, Mr. and Mrs. Average spend much less on clothing (only 63 percent of that reported in the CPI) and much more for health care (50 percent more than reported in the CPI).

A word or so of caution: If you attempt to refine the averages too much, you can actually distort them, to your disadvantage. It probably is better if you simply use the averages as presented by the government through the media. A perfectly true and valid argument can be made that each and every person will differ from the average, but by how much, in which direction, and during what time frame are simply impossible to determine with any degree of precision. Therefore, even though you may not be—and in fact are not—Mr. or Mrs. Average, using the average figures is good enough for most of your purposes.[3]

Remember: Your total income from all sources each year must increase by a percentage equal to that year's rate of inflation just for you to stay even. Anything less, and you fall behind and your standard of living will be affected.

notes

1. Fixed income is usually a level payment or income that does not change with time or inflation.

2. A recent change in how interest is computed for United States Savings Bonds is designed to address the problem of inflation.

3. The government is presently debating whether the CPI has actually over-stated true composite inflation by up to 1 percent. If a change is needed to better represent actual inflation, then I feel the CPI, as corrected, is still the best barometer available for our future planning.

chapter 4

Where the Money Goes

Daphne and Dudley Do-right are having an argument. It's about money. They have the same argument at the end of every month. Neither Daphne nor Dudley is sure why they never have enough money to pay all their bills. Each believes the other person is at fault. What they may not know is that money is one of the leading causes of divorce—and that there is a simple solution for their problem. It's called a budget.

Most people do not use a formal budget to ascertain their living expenses. In fact, most people look the other way at the mere mention of the word *budget*. However, it will become very clear to you after reading just a few chapters of this book that where you spend your money and how much you spend are the single most important factors in determining the kind of life you will live when you retire.

In 1992 I participated in a research program conducted by the Geriatrics Center of the University of Michigan. My interviewer was Dr. John Fink, gerontology researcher. When he realized that I was a financial consultant, he put down his interview papers and said, "If I had a magic wand, and I could have but one wish for all my patients, it would have nothing to do with medicine. It would be a wish for them to be financially well-off."

I didn't disagree, but this was a bit surprising coming from a medical doctor. Then he continued, "I believe that without my patients' worries and fears about the lack of money, much of their depression and anxiety would disappear and thereby eliminate many of their medical problems."

Dr. Walter Bortz II, author of *Dare to Be 100*, wrote, "Lack of financial resources is debilitating to morale—it leads to major health problems, which in turn only serve to make matters worse."

Once convinced of how important financial resources can be to their overall quality of life, most people are willing to at least look at where their money went. To do that, you must make a record. It is not always an easy task to prepare such a record, but if you follow these steps, it can be done with minimal pain.

Step One: Decide on the categories of expenditures you will use. See Appendix 1 for a suggested listing. There are also several money- or cash-flow-management software programs available that provide suggested listings of expense categories.

Step Two: Assemble your checkbook register and all your itemized charge-account statements for the past twelve months.

Step Three: Go through your checkbook register and charge-account statements and list the amount of each item under the proper expense category.

Step Four: This may be the hardest part. Allocate each *cash* purchase you made during the past twelve months to the proper expense category. If you do not have receipts or an accurate recollection of how much actual cash you spent, you will have to guess. In the future, you should keep a record of how much cash you receive and where it is spent. Do this by depositing *all* income into your checking account and then withdrawing cash as needed. You then will know how much cash you had to spend.

Next, if you save receipts for the big cash items, you probably will be able to guess at where the balance was spent (for example, so much a month for personal care, eating out per week or per month, gasoline, and other items paid for with cash). This activity alone will probably convince you to use as little cash as possible. It is much easier to track expenditures paid by check or credit cards. Of course, you should pay the complete monthly balance on each credit card within the grace period to avoid any and all interest charges.

Step Five: Find the sum of the amounts in each category and transfer the annual totals to a Cash Management Statement. (See Appendix 1 for a sample of this form.)

Now you are prepared for a retrospective analysis—a look back at how much you spent and where it went. You may find that certain amounts, even large ones, no longer represent your wants or needs, and without even using the word *budget*, you can alter future allocations in these categories. Now you also are ready to begin managing your money. But before you start, let's first take a peek into the future to see why you are doing all this work.

In the good old days, people commonly believed that they would have to reduce their standard of living during the retirement years. Today such beliefs are rare. Surveys show that almost no one expects to reduce his or her standard of living in retirement. And rather than spending just a few years in retirement, many people today can look forward to a very long period of retirement living. That is why you must learn to manage your money—to afford all this good retirement life.

Fifty-four percent of my clients are retired, and they all say the same thing: "Don, make my money last as long as I do, and I don't want to reduce my standard of living." Fortunately, these clients have saved some money. They did not wait until they were retired before they became concerned about funding their retirement years. What about you? Are you among those who hope to maintain their present standard of living during their retirement years? If so, do you know how much money you will need?

Two methods can be used to estimate how much money you will need in retirement. The first method is the *Replacement Ratio Method*. This method is used when actual retirement is not imminent. The second method is the *Actual Expense Method*. It is used when retirement is within a few years or has already commenced.

Replacement Ratio Method

You will need between 68 and 90 percent of your pre-retirement income to maintain the same standard of living after retirement. The actual percentage depends upon your level of pre-retirement income. If your current income is $60,000 or more in 2002 dollars, then 75 percent is an appropriate percentage to use. Use the higher percentage if your income is below $60,000. A sample calculation is shown below using 75 percent for a person currently earning $100,000 a year.

Income Required to Maintain the Same Standard of Living

Gross pre-retirement income	$100,000
Less income tax & Social Security tax	- $25,000
Less long-term savings	- $10,000
Net pre-retirement income	$65,000
Use appropriate percentage (68%–90%)	x 0.75
Net retirement income	$48,750
Plus income tax	+ $5,750
Gross retirement income	$54,500

A word of caution: The longer the period of time prior to actual retirement, the more your answer might be affected by changes in taxation, the rate of inflation, living standards improved by the ever-increasing applications of technology, and so forth.

Actual Expense Method

As you get close to your retirement date, more precise retirement income planning is required. This planning involves a change from the Replacement Ratio Method to the Actual Expense Method. The latter method requires you to make estimates of expected dollar outlays for each expense category.

For example, after retirement your work-related expenses will disappear and you can reallocate income spent on those expenses to other areas. But recognize that living expenses are a personal matter. Whether expenses in the other categories increase or decrease depends to a great extent on your personal choices and circumstances.

With all of the above in mind, here is a guide for preparing an expense statement. For each item, write your current annual expenditure. Then estimate the annual expenditure upon retirement.

Expenses that usually decrease are:

> Mortgage Payments (eventually eliminated)
> Food
> Clothing
> Taxes (income and Social Security)
> Debt Repayment (should be eliminated by now)
> Transportation
> Disability Income Insurance (probably eliminated)
> Life Insurance
> Household Furnishings
> Personal Care
> Medical and Medical Insurance (often reduces at age 65, but increases later)
> Savings and Investments

where the money goes

Expenses that usually increase are:
  Rent
  Property Tax
  House Upkeep (repairs and maintenance)
  Utilities and Telephone
  Auto, Home, and Liability Insurance
  Long-Term-Care Insurance
  Vacation and Travel
  Recreation and Entertainment
  Contributions and Gifts

After you retire, carefully track your actual expenses during the first year, and use that information to revise your projections for future expenses. Then closely monitor your budget annually, if not monthly. By doing this, you will note sometimes subtle, but always important, changes in sufficient time to make adjustments. For example, as one enters the later years of life, expenditures for entertainment extravagances might decrease as requirements for medical attention increase.

Let's review. We have been discussing proper money management, even to the point of knowing what we will need in years to come. Have you ever made a New Year's resolution about money? If you have, is it still working? If not, relax; you're not alone. Managing money is difficult because it is so personal, and there are no rules that are absolutely applicable to everyone. What we have been talking about is more than the management of money; it is the management of *you*. It is the management of how and why *you* spend *your* money.

Do you remember Daphne and Dudley Do-right? We met them at the beginning of this chapter. They were the couple on the verge of divorce over their money problems. Well, they have decided to save more money. They agree that one way is to be more selective in the supermarket by looking for similar quality but lower prices in off-brand or store-brand labels.

On the Do-right's next shopping trip, Dudley reaches for their usual brand of barbecued beans and pork rinds. Then he remembers their resolution. He replaces the product and selects Store Brand X. He looks at Daphne. She looks at Dudley. Their questions and emotions are evident in their eyes. Will the taste be the same? Is the nutrition the same? Did it undergo the same quality controls as their favored brand? She nods. He nods. Together, they carefully replace Store Brand X and pick up their usual brand. Their hands touching, they slowly and majestically drop it into their shopping cart. Fade music. Bring up lights.

Although movies usually end at this point, in real life Daphne and Dudley return home frustrated, angry, and definitely ready to give up the whole idea of trying to change their spending habits. Rather than do this, however, they should sit down and review exactly what happened. They should realize that they are only victims of the way their minds have been programmed. They are not failures at money management. They simply need more practice. This means, try again.

Money management is affected by your attitudes, emotions, and habits. The old ways of doing things rarely ever change simply by making a resolution, even if it is a joint resolution. Change occurs only when you resolve to try different ways to do things or when it is thrust upon you. The latter offers you no choice; you must change. The former, although it might be a difficult change to make, is easier because you get to try, try, and try again.

Resolve to make minor changes in categories you know you must change. This gradual adjustment in your life is easier to make than, say, being thrown into cold water and commanded to swim. Take the Do-rights and the barbecued beans and pork rinds. They have many choices, but they are more comfortable selecting the brand they know instead of trying the unknown.

Recognize that you probably are no different than the Do-rights. What often starts out with a resolution to change your money habits often ends with what appears to be money-management failure. You should not berate yourself for this lapse. Learn from it. Then try again. Remember, your financial future will be greatly enhanced if you stick to your goals.

It's your money. There is no reason why you cannot manage it the way you want except for bad habits. You did not inherit these bad habits. They were not genetically determined. You learned them. So learn new habits, good habits. One way you might do this is to write down what you spend.

As part of the preparation for a complete health evaluation at the Cooper Clinic in Dallas, Texas, patients are asked to write down everything they eat for three consecutive days. Do you know what happens if you do this? You become very conscious of what you put into your mouth. When you know someone is going to scrutinize everything you eat, you have second thoughts about overeating or eating food that you know you should not have. You are more aware of your diet. In the same way, you can become more aware of how you spend your money. Write it down.

Get a little notebook to carry with you. Write in this note-book each and every amount you spend and what you spend it for. As you do this, you become more aware of where your money goes. The real key to money management is to know how you spend your money. Your little notebook will be of more help than you might think. It will tell you how you spent the cash portion of your hard-earned money. You won't have to wonder. You won't have to guess. You won't have to assume. When you list expenditures from your checkbook, charge accounts, and your notebook, you know where your money goes.

Quite a few years ago I completed a physical examination that revealed my total cholesterol had increased from 196 to 225. This was quite disappointing to me considering my attitude about health habits. I asked my doctor why it went up. He said, "Well, maybe you have slipped on controlling your fat intake." Indignant at such a suggestion, I responded, "No way! I'm very careful!" He looked at me for a moment and then just shrugged his shoulders. That was a challenge, so for three months I wrote down every item I put in my mouth and recorded the grams of fat involved. At the end of the three months, I had my cholesterol rechecked. It was 191.

I was most pleased, of course, but I also knew that I owed my doctor an apology. He was right. I really had slipped on controlling the fat grams I consumed. The only difference between the three months prior to my first visit and the three months prior to my second visit was that, the second time around, I wrote it down.

The only way to really know is to write it down. Do this for one year using a Cash Management Statement form for the annual summary. At least once a month for a year, list all expenditures under their proper categories. Transfer the amounts from your check register, from your credit card and other receipts, and from your little notebook. At the end of the year, match the totals of all categories against your estimated amounts for these categories. Then adjust the figures for future allocations according to your needs and wants. This time, because you know where you spent every dollar last year, you will make more accurate estimates for future expenditures.

Until you write it down, you are managing money in the dark, and you risk the possibility of financial mismanagement. When you write it down, you are on the road to effective money management—the first step to financial success. You now are in control of your money.

Keeping records of actual expenditures in your first year of retirement is especially valuable. Your outlay does change in retirement, and even though it is recommended that you estimate these changes when you use the Actual Expense Method, having an accurate expense record will improve your estimates and will provide very solid information when you prepare your Retirement Cash Flow Analysis in Chapter 9. If you already are retired, I still recommend that you keep a record of actual expenses for a twelve-month period. The management of your money for the balance of your life will be much improved.

Developing a Cash Management Statement

1. Prepare a list of categories for all expenditures. (See Appendix 1.)

2. Assemble your checkbook register and charge-account statements.

3. Transfer each item in #2 into the proper category in #1.

4. Allocate all cash expenditures to the proper category in #1.

5. Find the total for each category and transfer the totals to a Cash Management Statement. (See Appendix 1.)

For some of you, especially those who have the whole process on their computers, this process will be a piece of cake. The remainder of you may be wondering if you really should put up with all this pain. The answer is an emphatic *Yes*; the significance of an accurate Cash Management Statement should not be minimized. My clients pay me a lot of money to be their financial advisor, and the first thing I tell each of them to do is prepare a Cash Management Statement. This becomes the foundation upon which the client's financial future is built.

When I review a Cash Management Statement for a client, I look first at the bottom line—the total expenditures—and compare this with total income. Of course, it doesn't take a genius to recognize whether there is an excess of income over expenditure or—perish the thought!—the opposite.

If more is going out than coming in, then you are mimicking the federal government and are incurring debt. During the twentieth century, the United States government had a budget surplus-to-deficit ratio of 32 to 68; that is, from 1901 through 2000, the government had a budget surplus during only thirty-two years. During the other sixty-eight years, the government had a budget deficit. During the second half of the twentieth century, there were only eight surplus years, and for thirty years from 1971 through 2000, there were only three surplus years.

Since the federal government has the power to increase taxes anytime it wants to cover its excessive spending, it can get away with this improper money management. But if you continue to mimic the government year after year, you will find yourself spending an increasing percentage of your income on interest charges. For some unfortunate people, this situation is a sink-hole from which there is no escape. If this is the path you are currently on, then recognize where it is taking you and do something immediately to change direction.

If you have been spending more than you are receiving and have consequently accumulated extensive consumer debt—this is all debt except the mortgage on your residence—then it would be in your best interest to seriously consider the following formula. I learned this formula when reading a wonderful little book titled *The Richest Man in Babylon*, by George S. Clason. To paraphrase, for every dollar that represents your take-home pay—what you have after income tax and Social Security tax have been deducted or otherwise accounted for—you must:

- First, set aside 10 percent in long-term savings;

- Next, allocate 20 percent to the reduction and eventual elimination of debt;

- Then live on the remaining 70 percent.

Of course, living on 70 percent of your after-tax income means that you must use this money to pay for any and all new charges you make as soon as you receive the statement. Said differently, NO NEW DEBT!

Yes, this may be harsh medicine, but the bitter taste will go away just as your debt will go away. Let me assure you, living debt-free is a feeling like few other feelings you have had. When you have debt, it is a heavy weight that has all kinds of negative effects on your health, your relations with others, and your own self-image. When you are debt-free, you really are free from more than just debt. There is no better way to live. But more than your newfound freedom from debt, you now have an additional 20 percent of your take-home pay to use to increase your standard of living and/or to become wealthier sooner. Get debt-free, live better, and have more!

Second, I look for categories with large allocations. A larger-than-normal amount might be proper because the way you spend your money is absolutely unique to you. However, it is important for you to understand what you are doing, and why, so that you can make proper adjustments in other categories. It is possible that an allocation to a specific category has simply gotten out of hand and does not really represent your current needs or desires.

Next, I look for items that might represent opportunities for either savings or for increased spending to better match your desires. Some people find it difficult to accept that a Cash Management Statement can show a surplus that needs to be reallocated—that is, spent. I see this most often with retirees. The surplus is great news to them, of course, but it is very difficult to get them to be more comfortable spending more money. Their fear of running out of money before running out of life is over-powering, and we will discuss this in greater detail later.

Finally, clients who have prepared a Cash Management Statement for at least a few years prior to retirement have a somewhat easier time doing what I call "playing retirement." This is where we add a right-hand column to the Cash Manage-ment Statement titled Retirement. Then we change the current year's figures to an estimate of what they will be in retirement. Even though this activity involves estimates, it still becomes an excellent source to use when we prepare a Retirement Cash Flow Analysis. Close estimates are very important. When you project inflation rates and investment rates of return over many years, the compounding of these estimated numbers will greatly exaggerate any inaccuracies.

There you have it, the how and why of keeping a record of all expenditures.

chapter 5

Managing Your Money

As Charles Dickens tells us in *David Copperfield*, "Annual income twenty pounds, annual expenditure nineteen six, result happiness. Annual income twenty pounds, annual expenditure twenty pounds ought and six, result misery." Then, as now, a wise person knows that for happiness you must spend less than you make.

How you use your money is a very personal matter, and no one can tell you how you must allocate it. You will decide what you will buy and when. However, if your expenditures exceed your income, you should welcome some professional advice.

You will manage your retirement money more effectively if you are properly managing your money before you retire. If you are not doing this now, changes are in order.

Changing does not require you to turn your world upside down. What it does require, as a first step, is that you become aware of what you currently are doing with your money. (See Chapter 4 for details on developing a Cash Management Statement.) Then, after a proper review, you can decide what adjustments you need to make. In this way, by the time you retire, you should have a good handle on the best way to allocate your money. Otherwise, it could be increasingly more difficult to maintain a desirable standard of living once your wage-earning days are over.

How you manage your money prior to retirement will in large part determine what you have to spend in the early years of retirement. And because it is quite possible that you will live thirty or forty years after you retire, the amount you spend in the early years of retirement will have an enormous effect on your standard of living in later years.

What should you know and do prior to retirement? First, make it an annual practice to list all expenditures for the preceding year. Then you can make adjustments that best meet your current needs. Many people are quite surprised to find that certain expenditures, maybe even large ones, are no longer important, while other expenditures have become more essential.

It is not unusual for people to continue spending on things that have outlived their usefulness to them. When you were a young family and had to transport your children and their friends all over town, you may have driven a van or SUV. Are you still driving that vehicle even though your kids are now approaching their forties? Perhaps another type of vehicle would be both a better fit for your present needs, and more economical.

Here are some other questions to ask. Are you still renewing publications that you no longer read? Are you maintaining memberships in groups that no longer interest to you? How many of your season tickets go unused or are given away? An annual review should raise many questions like these, and the answers will help you think about reallocating some funds.

The earlier you start analyzing the way you manage your income, the more likely you will enjoy the life you really desire. Also, the more likely you will be able to accumulate the funds necessary for maintaining that lifestyle in the future, right through your retirement years.

Before Retirement

Before retirement, there are basically only two controlling factors: how much you earn and how much you spend. Although you might have some control over your income, you probably have much more control over how that income, whatever it may be, is allocated. Many people begin their planning by using the average household allocation of income as a benchmark. This data is shown in the circle graph below.

Allocation of After-Tax Income

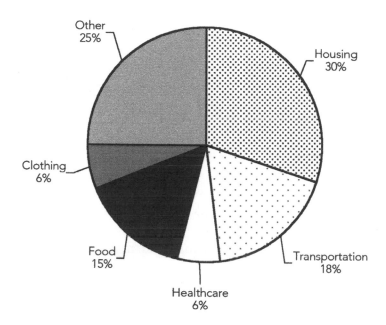

As you can see, 75 percent of the average household's net income—that is, income after taxes, or what is sometimes called take-home pay—goes to pay for the basics: 15 percent for food, 6 percent for clothing, 30 percent for housing, 18 percent for transportation (including vehicles), and 6 percent for health care. Compare your own spending to these averages. Do these basics absorb more than three-quarters of your income? If they do, you may be missing a lot of the more pleasant things in life such as entertainment, personal care, and pleasure trips. Also included in the "Others" category is long-term accumulations and debt repayment.[1]

If you are spending more than 75 percent of your income on the basics, examine the reasons why. First, determine what percent of your income goes to each of the basics.[2] If you have an excessive allocation to any category, re-evaluate the importance of those expenditures. Is it really necessary or desirable, for example, to pay so much per month to lease that "special" automobile? Remember, if too much of your income goes to one category, the funds available for other categories are reduced. The sum of all categories should equal your total income.

Since the basics require about 75 percent of your net income, and since these moneys are all for immediate expenses, you next need to look seriously at how you will allocate the remaining 25 or so percent of your income. To do this properly, you also must look into the future. When will big-ticket purchases occur? How much time do you have to accumulate the necessary funds for these items? How much time do you have to accumulate money for the college education you want for your children? How much time do you have to save for the comfortable retirement you want? Determine what your answers are to these and similar questions and make your plans accordingly.

One obstacle many consumers face is the need to spend a large part of their income on consumer-debt repayments. If you are one of these consumers, I strongly recommend that you bite the bullet immediately. As stated in Chapter 4, apply 20 percent of your income to repaying this debt. Make the temporary sacrifices that are necessary. Don't incur new debt. Then at some future date, probably two years or less for most debtors, you will be debt-free and can apply that 20 percent to your needs and desires.

Remember this maxim: Time is the secret to accumulating more funds for retirement. The longer your savings and investments accumulate and grow, the better off you will be. And if you haven't started that process, the time to begin is now.

After Retirement

Until they retire, most people earn money and live on it. First comes the cash flow, or earnings, and then comes the budget, written or not, that guides how to live within that cash flow. With a good budget, they will spend no more than they earn. At retirement, this procedure is reversed. First comes the desired standard of living, or budget, and then comes the creation of the money to pay for it. This reversal is important to produce and maintain the desired standard of living in retirement and also to keep taxation under control.

Pretend that you are a new client of mine, and you have just retired. The first thing we would do together is to determine how much cash flow you need or desire. Then we would create that cash flow.

We would start by listing all income that is not under your control, such as Social Security and employer pension plans. Then we would compare that total with the amount required to cover your desired standard of living. For some, there is already sufficient or excess cash flow. If this is true in your case, we would be in the wonderful position of being able to raise your standard of living, create a gifting program, or simply keep wealth invested in high-growth investments for future use.

More often than not, there is a shortfall. In that case, we would review your investment portfolio to find the most propitious places to create the additional cash flow, but only the amount needed. Excess income would likely create excess income tax, which in turn would reduce your ability to make your money last as long as you do.

Ironically, good pre-retirement habits can follow you into retirement to become bad retirement habits. You have spent a lifetime trying to "live within your means" and save at least some of your earnings. When we try to change this procedure, it can take some time for you to adjust. I often have newly retired clients come in during the first few years of their retirement boasting about how much money they have saved "even in retirement."

"That's terrible!" I tell these clients, pointing out that such excess cash inflow probably created excess income tax. I ask, "Why do you want to give 10 percent or more as a gift to the government?" What you should do is create only the income that you need and let the rest grow—tax-deferred for those investments within retirement plans, such as IRAs—until it's needed. If ever you want to increase your standard of living, simply create more inflow.

There is no doubt that it's difficult to change habits learned over a lifetime. My oldest client, for example, was still very alert and mobile when she was 94. One day I asked Isabelle, "Is there anything that you need or want?"

"Nothing," she replied almost automatically. I inquired several more times during this meeting because she had more than sufficient assets to provide for her current standard of living and could well afford some extras. So, one last time, I asked, "Are you sure there isn't something that would be nice to have?"

"Well," she started, and then hesitated.

"Yes?" I prodded once more.

"Well," she finally admitted, "I don't have air conditioning in my Florida condo, and it would be nice. But I spend a lot of time up north here, and I really don't have to have it."

"Isabelle," I said, "do you have forced air heat in your condo?"

"Yes," she replied.

"Do you realize how little it would cost to add air conditioning to your heating system?" I asked. I proceeded to estimate what it might cost, and it was definitely a small, non-extravagant expenditure for her. Isabelle died one year after our conversation. She left her few heirs what many would consider a small fortune. Her assets included her Florida condo, without air conditioning.

Another day I received an out-of-state call from Doug. "Don," he said, "I've always wanted a Lincoln, and I need a new car. Can I afford a Lincoln?" Doug was in his early eighties and in poor health. He was not extremely rich, but he had plenty of income and assets to serve him and his wife well for at least twenty and probably thirty more years.

"Of course you can afford a Lincoln," I told him.

One month later, Doug called again. "Are you sure I can afford a Lincoln?"

I immediately and emphatically responded, "Yes!" Doug had made only a fairly good living, but he and his wife lived on less than his income for many years. The old expression describes it best: He "squirreled away" money that a person desiring a higher standard of living would have spent.

Another month went by, and I received another call from Doug. He asked the same question and I gave the same reply. A couple of weeks later, he called again. I started to say yes before he asked the question, but this time he stopped me when he said, "Don, I bought a new car."

"Wonderful!" I said. "What color is your new Lincoln?"

"Oh, I didn't buy a Lincoln," Doug said. "They're too expensive."

Role reversals are hard at any age. They are especially difficult at older ages because they involve ingrained habits. But such role reversals at retirement are just one of the many changes you will be called upon to make just to keep up with the ever-changing world.

notes

1. Mortgage payments are included in "Housing." The debt repayments discussed here are what we call consumer debts such as credit card balances and store or bank loans for large-item purchases.

2. To find the percent, divide the amount you spend on the category by the total amount of your net income. Move the decimal point in the answer two places to the right. For example, if the net income is $1,400 and $175 is spent in the food category, then the percent is 175 ÷ 1400 = 0.125 = 12.5 percent.

chapter 6

Projecting Your Lifetime Financial Needs

Jan and John Justus plan to retire in ten years. They both are wise enough to know that a lot can happen before they retire. They still remember their grandparents' stories about the Great Depression. They also remember, because they lived through it, a period of hyperinflation in which the inflation rate reached double-digit numbers—12.2 percent in 1974, 13.3 percent in 1979, and 12.4 percent in 1980. They wonder if it is even possible to know how much money they will need to retire.

John says, "We have gone over the figures. We even used the Replacement Ratio Method (see Chapter 4) to determine that we need an annual income of $54,500. But that's in today's dollars, and I'm worried about how inflation might affect this number over a ten-year period."

Jan suggests, "Suppose we assume an average inflation rate of 3 percent for each of the ten years. Then we can use a financial calculator to find the amount of income we will need."

Jan and John calculated the results and came up with $73,243 as the annual income they would need to maintain their financial status and fulfill their plans.[1] With some minor changes here and there, they decided that they would be able to generate this amount of income from various sources. To celebrate, they each had a dish of no-fat ice cream covered with no-calorie chocolate syrup.

It is unfortunate that Jan and John Justus made a major error at this point in their planning. Most young people do. They believe that when they have determined the gross retirement income figure adjusted for inflation, they are all set. The figure for Jan and John is $73,243. However, this figure is the amount they expect to need in the *first* year of retirement only. Unless inflation disappears the moment they retire, their income need will continue to increase each year for the remainder of their lives. For example, continuing to assume the average rate of inflation at 3 percent, they will need $73,243 plus 3 percent of $73,243, or $75,440 the second year of retirement. They will need $75,440 plus 3 percent of $75,440, or $77,703 the third year. And so it will go.

Keep in mind that the 3 percent as an average rate of inflation is an assumption. The actual rate could be 5 percent or more. Take a peek at the chart for the annual amounts needed through the age of one hundred for our Justus couple at inflation rates of 3 percent and 5 percent. Keep in mind that with proper investments your assets should also increase in value.

Should you want to make a similar list for a different rate of inflation, the calculations are relatively easy, although tedious. Suppose you assume an average inflation rate of 4 percent. Start with your original required income, like the Justus's $73,243. Multiply the amount by 1.04, and the result is the next year's required income.[2] Continue to multiply the new amount by 1.04 to get the following year's amount. Those of you who are familiar with computers and spreadsheet programs can easily use one to avoid the tedium.

Projecting income needs over many years is subject to many unknowns and should not be considered foolproof. In fact, you should assume that any such projection is inaccurate. This is why you might want to make different assumptions when generating data. This is called the "what if" approach to life's uncertainty. For example, we just asked and answered, "What if the annual rate of inflation is 3 percent?" and "What if it is 5 percent?" You have been given the mathematical tools to ask "what if" for any other rate you wish to assume.

Although long-term projections may be inaccurate, they are still better than wandering into the future completely unprepared. For one thing, our projections for the Justus couple showed that at 3 percent inflation the income they would need will double in about twenty-four years. And if the average rate of inflation is 5 percent, the required income will double in only fifteen years.

Required Annual Income at 3% and 5% Inflation

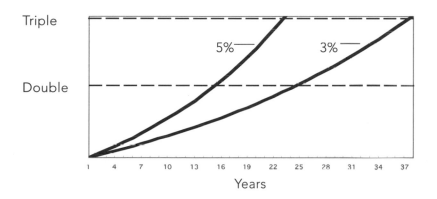

At 3% inflation, the income required for retirement doubles in 24 years and triples in 38 years. At 5% inflation, the amount doubles in 15 years and triples in 23 years.

If you have absorbed these simple but astounding facts, then welcome to the enlightened few. Not many people today recognize how inflation can ravage their best-laid plans for comfort during retirement. Now you do.

Here is a worthwhile exercise: Use what you learned in Chapter 4 to estimate the annual income you will need when you retire. Then assume an average rate of inflation of 2 percent and show what you will need in each of your forty-plus years of retirement. Then do a "what if" and make another list to show what you will need in each of those years if the average rate of inflation is 8 percent. In all likelihood you've just constructed the best-case and worst-case scenarios for your retirement. Be aware, however, that even this exercise carries no guarantees because 2 percent and 8 percent do not represent the lowest and highest rates of inflation in our history.

No one can predict the future, including this author. But if you learn nothing else from this book, you should come to understand that with the proper concepts and skills shown here, you will have a greater mastery of your future financial health.

At this point you have calculated what you will need as income the year you retire and in the years following retirement at different assumed rates of inflation. You have only just begun. Since you will grow smarter as you grow older, and information available to you also will change, you should plan to revise your plans annually. Change is inevitable. Your income estimates may change if, for example, you decide to return to work part-time or start a consulting business. Likewise, your expenses may change if, say, you decide to move to a smaller home or are hit with a sudden case of wanderlust and want to travel more frequently. The possibilities are endless. The important thing is that you take them into account and plan accordingly. As I've said, retirement should be what you want it to be, not what financial circumstances dictate.

Later in the book, we will do similar projections for Social Security, private and company pensions, and other possible income sources. We also will present projections of future investment results. Hazardous as projecting may be, such projections are the best way to look ahead simply because we have not found a consistently reliable crystal ball that gives a perfect picture of the future.

In the past, projecting for five years gave fairly dependable results. Today, projecting for five months is questionable. Could five-day projections eventually become hazardous to your wealth? Before you say "nonsense," remember that some countries of South America had a history of inflation rates so high that their citizens actually lost purchasing power on the way to the store. Can this book guarantee that you will not suffer the fate of those shoppers? Not likely. But it will arm you with the weapons of knowledge that will be your best defense against a worst-case scenario and help you reap more benefits during a best-case scenario.

notes

1. The Justus couple used a financial calculator that displayed the decimal as 1.343916379. Using this precise (but still rounded) decimal yields the amount $73,243.

2. The number 1.04 is the decimal for 104 percent. The 100 percent is the original amount; the 4 percent is the assumed rate of inflation. You could find the next year's amount by multiplying the current amount by 0.04 and adding the result to the current amount. Multiplying the current amount by 1.04 gives the same answer in one step.

chapter 7

The Wobbly Three-Legged Stool of Retirement Income

When Paul Persons retired, he announced it to his wife, Paula, by coming through the kitchen door one night saying, "I've had enough. One more day on this job, and I'll have a heart attack. Or worse."

Paula had been expecting something like this. She had watched Paul come home from work more upset each day for the past year or more after his company downsized.

"I mean it, Paula," Paul continued. "If you want me around for a while longer, then know that I'm not going back."

Paula nodded. She was not really surprised, but she had hoped that Paul could stick it out for two more years, until his Social Security would start. But she knew Paul was right. The requirements of his job had changed, and she had watched how the increasing pressures had begun to affect Paul's health. No, she was not really surprised, but she knew that neither of them was really prepared, either. What would replace Paul's paycheck?

Paul and Paula started their research the next day. First, they met with a person in the retirement department of Paul's employer. Although they walked away with more questions than answers, they did have the assurance that Paul qualified for an immediate monthly pension benefit.

Next, they visited the local Social Security office. Then they visited their life-insurance specialist, followed by their stock-broker, and finally an excellent financial consultant. All, in one way or another, gave them pertinent information.

The Persons learned that the traditional sources of retirement income are still valid. Their financial consultant also told them that the traditional three-legged-stool model was still applicable. "The what?" they asked. They had never heard of such a thing. In response, they got a history lesson.

Back in the 1930s, the U.S. government accepted a role as a retirement-income provider. The program, enacted in 1935 during the Great Depression, was Social Security. Unfortunately for Paul and Paula, the benefits from Social Security were two years away. Back in the 1950s, employers became more involved as a retirement-income source. After 1974, when the federal law ERISA[1] was enacted, the popularity of individual retirement planning increased. Over the ensuing years, individuals took advantage of the new law by allocating more and more of their personal resources to long-term-accumulation programs, most of which were tax-deferred.

Paul and Paula Persons recognized how fortunate they were that Paul's employer participated in a retirement program authorized under ERISA. They also began to understand how it has evolved that most people look (1) to the government Social Security program, (2) to their employer's retirement plan, and (3) to their own personal wealth as the three sources of retirement income. This, they realized, is the three-legged-stool model. One leg is the federal government, the second leg is a company retirement plan, and the third leg is the individual's own retirement plan. The Persons also recognized that the amount that comes from each rarely equals either of the other two amounts. In other words, the legs on this stool are not of equal size.

After several meetings with their financial consultant, Paul and Paula learned the following guides for the three sources of retirement income.

The Three Sources of Retirement Income

Sources	Replacement Ratio Ranges[2]
Government Social Security	5% up to 60%
Employer Pension Plan	0% up to 50%
Personal Wealth Accumulation	The Balance

Here's an example. Suppose, using one of the methods described in Chapter 4, you determine the income you will need in retirement. You learn that Social Security in your case will supply 26 percent of this needed income. You also learn that your company pension will supply 50 percent of this needed income. So far, these two legs of the stool will supply you with 26 + 50 or 76 percent of your needed income. You still need 100 − 76, or 24 percent. This 24 percent must come from the third leg of the stool, your own personal wealth accumulation.

Social Security

To determine how much retirement income you might need from your employer pension plan and personal wealth accumulation, first determine what part of this income would be provided by your Social Security retirement benefit.

The dollar amount of retirement benefits you receive from Social Security is based on the amount of earnings on which you paid FICA tax.[3] To be eligible for retirement benefits, you must have at least ten years of work covered by Social Security. The amount you will receive is based on the thirty-five years of your highest earnings. This amount is applied to a formula to determine the actual monthly benefit. If a spouse's benefit, based on his or her benefit as determined by the formula, is less than one-half the amount for which he or she would qualify from his or her spouse's benefit, then the larger amount is paid.

You can obtain a report of your status free of charge by calling the Social Security Administration at 800-772-1213 and requesting the required form to obtain this information. The Web address is *www.ssa.gov*. Statements are being sent unsolicited to workers age 25 or older prior to every birthday.

Social Security produces a wide range in the replacement ratios, mostly due to two factors. The first is the amount of average pre-retirement income earned. The second is your personal status: single, married with a spouse qualifying for full benefit, or married with a spouse qualifying for a portion of the working spouse's benefit.

The following chart illustrates the Social Security replacement ratios for a single worker and a couple, all age 62.

Social Security Replacement Ratios

Pre-Retirement Income	Both Spouses Qualify for Maximum Individual Benefits	One Spouse Qualifies for Maximum Benefit; Other Receives a Spousal Benefit	Single Qualifier
$20,000	60%	45%	31%
$40,000	47%	35%	24%
$60,000	35%	26%	18%
$80,000	26%	19%	13%
$100,000	21%	16%	11%
$150,000	14%	10%	7%
$200,000	11%	8%	5%

The chart makes several things obvious. First, the lower your pre-retirement income, the higher your Social Security replacement ratio. Second, the higher your pre-retirement income, the more you should plan to replace income through one of the other two legs of your three-legged stool. Finally, regardless of pre-retirement income, a single qualifier will need the vast majority of retirement income from sources other than Social Security.

In Chapter 4 we learned that many people need about 75 percent of their pre-retirement income to maintain the same standard of living in retirement. But for pre-retirement incomes below $60,000 (in year 2002 dollars), the needed retirement income rises to as high as 90 percent. Regardless of your pre-retirement income or your desired standard of living in retirement, Social Security will not provide all the income you will need in retirement. The Social Security Administration clearly states in many of its publications: "Social Security is not designed to meet all your future financial needs. You need additional sources of income."

Social Security benefits are currently adjusted each year to maintain the purchasing power of this income. This adjustment is based on the inflation rate for the preceding year (a year is from October through the following September). The concept is fairly easy to understand. If the cost of living increased 3.5 percent in the preceding year, and the benefit for that year was $10,000, then the benefit for this year will be $10,350.[4] Because each inflation adjustment is applied to the preceding year's dollar amount, the adjustments made year after year are considered the same as compounded, and they fairly accurately reflect the amounts needed to keep the income stream on a par with inflation. However, there is a strong probability that a percentage rate less than the actual inflation rate will be applied in the future.

Employer Retirement Plans

Employer retirement plans are already going through a great metamorphosis. They are changing to quasi-employer plans. That is, more and more of the assets of these plans come from a salary reduction for the employee.[5]

Often in the past, an employer made all the contributions to the retirement plan. Now the popular 401(k) plan often involves only a partial contribution from the employer. Some plans involve a matching employer contribution where, for example, the employer contributes a dollar to the plan for each dollar contributed by an employee. Other plans involve only a percentage of the employee contribution—a dollar contribution from the employer for, say, each two dollars contributed by the employee. Employers also often limit their participation to a maximum percentage of wages, usually from 3 to 6 percent. If your employer has a 5 percent limit and your yearly income is $30,000, the employer will match up to $1,500 of your contributions to the plan. That is, $30,000 times .05 equals $1,500.

It is critically important where the contributions are invested. Unfortunately, more than one-quarter of the participants may be investing in the wrong type of account. This important issue is discussed in greater detail in Chapter 10.

Unlike Social Security, the vast majority of employer retirement plans do not have a cost-of-living annual adjustment. As you saw in Chapter 6, your retirement budget must increase each year there is inflation in this country, which you can expect most of the years of your retirement. Without an inflation adjustment in an employer pension plan, the amount you receive from this plan will replace a smaller percentage of your required income each year. You must then rely more on the other two legs of your retirement income stool.

A few employer plans have an annual increase in benefits based on a fixed dollar amount. This is considered simple as compared to compounded. This dollar adjustment is better than nothing, but each year it becomes of less significance. The Michigan Public School Employees Retirement System has such a benefit, and we can use it as an example here. For those participants who elected to contribute approximately 4 percent of their income to the plan, an annual increase of 3 percent of the first year's retirement income benefit is added each year. The following listing compares this increase—3 percent simple, shown in the middle column—with 3 percent compounded, shown in the right-hand column.

Simple Interest Compared to Compound Interest

Year	Simple	Compounded
1	$10,000	$10,000
2	10,300	10,300
3	10,600	10,609
4	10,900	10,927
5	11,200	11,255
6	11,500	11,593
7	11,800	11,941
8	12,100	12,299
9	12,400	12,668
10	12,700	13,048
11	13,000	13,439
12	13,300	13,842
13	13,600	14,258
14	13,900	14,685
15	14,200	15,126
16	14,500	15,580
17	14,800	16,047
18	15,100	16,528
19	15,400	17,024
20	15,700	17,535

Year	Simple	Compounded
21	$16,000	$18,061
22	16,300	18,603
23	16,600	19,161
24	16,900	19,736
25	17,200	20,328
26	17,500	20,938
27	17,800	21,566
28	18,100	22,213
29	18,400	22,879
30	18,700	23,566
31	19,000	24,273
32	19,300	25,001
33	19,600	25,751
34	19,900	26,523
35	20,200	27,319
36	20,500	28,139
37	20,800	28,983
38	21,100	29,852
39	21,400	30,748
40	21,700	31,670

Personal Wealth Accumulation

Personal wealth accumulation will be necessary to produce the balance of retirement income you desire. Social Security will be in serious trouble in the future due to substantial increases in benefits based on higher average earnings, the built-in inflation adjustments to the benefits, and the great number of baby boomers who will begin entering the program in just a few years. To save the program, the government makes adjustments. They already have increased many times the amount of income on which you must pay Social Security taxes. Now they have nowhere else to go except to tinker with the benefits, and the age at which you can begin enjoying benefits. The first leg of our three-legged stool is a bit wobbly.

As noted earlier, employers already have reduced their contributions to pensions, and there is no reason to expect this trend to reverse its direction. The second leg of our three-legged stool also is a bit unstable.

The obvious conclusion is that each of us must become more self-reliant. Personal wealth accumulation—the third leg of our stool—has become extremely important. No matter when you start to invest a portion of your earnings, it cannot be too soon.[6] It can be difficult for those in their twenties and thirties to set aside anything, but no matter how difficult it is, try to save 10 percent of all take-home pay if you are in this age group. How much is 10 percent? Simply take your paycheck dollar amount, mentally move the decimal point one place to the left, and invest this amount. For example, if your paycheck shows $510.00, you should invest $51.00.

Yes, it may be difficult to save 10 percent of your net income, particularly when you are starting a family and trying to buy a house. But if you start, it soon will become a habit, and then it will be easy. Just pretend that this 10 percent is a bill that must be paid first. Pay it to yourself. You've earned it.

When you enter your forties, this amount should be increased to 10 percent of your gross income.[7] Then in your fifties and sixties you should strive to double the amount you have been saving.

Working

I am becoming increasingly uncomfortable with the three-legged stool as the model of money forever. As we've seen, this model stands on uneven legs, two of which are becoming wobblier every day. In addition, outside circumstances can quickly change whatever balance you may achieve and destabilize your money supply.

One solution to potential future changes is to maintain a considerable reserve of assets that could be called upon when needed. This excess wealth will provide the necessary peace of mind and allow adjustments to the many life changes that accompany an extended period of life after working. Many people, however, are not able to develop this excess wealth. The next-best solution seems to be continued full- or part-time work. Perhaps preparing for your "retirement" should include mapping a plan for a secondary career.

Surveys of baby boomers indicate that 80 percent say they plan to work after their normal working years. They may know something their elders did not, or perhaps the older baby boomers simply realize that the amount of net worth they have accumulated will not maintain their desired standard of living if they stop working.

Work After Retirement

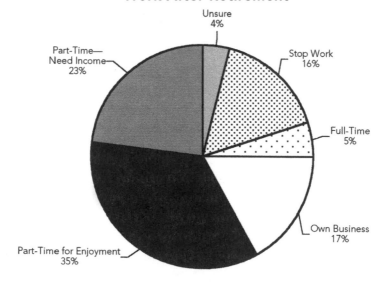

Source: AARP by Roper Starch Worldwide Inc.

Another compelling argument for continuing employment beyond the usual retirement age is that you are not ready to walk away from the many satisfactions provided by a work environment. If you don't like your job, it might be quite difficult to fathom such a thought. But if you really do like and look forward to the daily activities of your job, I'm sure it is conceivable that you would entertain a postponement of nonwork if it is an option offered to you.

The United Nations declared 1999 the International Year of Older Persons and developed eighteen principles, one of which reads, "Older persons should be able to participate in determining when and at what pace withdrawal from the labor force takes place."

Many years ago I read the book *Don't Ever Retire But Do It Early and Often,* by Joseph Schwartz. The author's point was to enjoy the different talents you possess. Try new things. Just make sure you enjoy what you are doing. I have a client who retired after thirty years of teaching and took a job in a hardware store. He told me how happy he was. "I finally found something I am good at and enjoy almost all the time I'm doing it," he said.

If you are considering early retirement, there is a side effect you must consider carefully. When you take early retirement, you elect to receive reduced Social Security benefits. If you decide to return to employment that pays over the maximum allowed by Social Security for early retirees, up to age 65 you will lose some or all of your Social Security income for as long as you remain employed. Later, when you return to full-time retirement again, your Social Security benefit is locked in at the reduced percentage you elected the first time you retired.

Take the case of Tad Early. Tad finally made it to age 62, exclaiming, "That's it. I've had enough." He felt burned out and believed that if he didn't retire, he would die from the stress. Whether this was true or merely a rationalization to justify ending his stressful career really doesn't matter. Tad Early made the decision and retired.

Tad made the obligatory trip to the Social Security office to get the ball rolling. He learned that starting benefits at age 62, he would receive a reduced benefit of only 80 percent of what he could receive if he waited to age 65 to retire. (See Appendix 2 for information on larger reductions for people born after 1937.) Since Tad had made up his mind and he needed the money in order to retire, he requested that his Social Security benefits begin.

Tad played golf for the next five months, five or more days a week. His blood pressure went down. His physical complaints started to disappear as his stress level decreased. He began to feel great. At this point, Tad thought, "There must be more to life than playing golf, particularly since I'm feeling so healthy." He even began to tire of golf—unthinkable when he first retired.

Tad started to attend community functions, seniors' meetings, and so on. What he learned there was that quite a few retired seniors need assistance in personal money management. Tad's many years as a financial officer with his former employer made it easy for him to serve only a short apprenticeship with his own financial consultant.

He found that the combination of his experience and his renewed education positioned him to provide a much-needed service to other retirees. By the first anniversary of his retirement, Tad was employed full-time and making more money than he did prior to retirement. Of course this disqualified him for Social Security benefits, and they stopped.

For the next two years, Tad enjoyed this new, personally rewarding occupation. It not only added money to his budget, but it also added a strong and rewarding feeling of giving back to the community. Then at age 65, he decided he would like to stop the daily trips to the office. He also felt that a year or two of research would enable him to write a book on the subject of money management. So Tad retired again.

He received a big surprise when he made the trip back to the Social Security office. The re-establishment of his Social

Security benefit was easy, but it would still be at the 80 percent level he had received three years earlier. He argued that he was 65 now and entitled to a full benefit. It was all to no avail. He was locked into that percentage for life.

The moral of Tad's story: Before you decide to take early retirement and elect a reduced Social Security benefit, make sure that you understand that you will always receive a reduced benefit, whether or not you return to full employment. The rule is different if you start benefits at the full or nonreduced benefit level. If you retire at or after the time when you qualify for full benefits and then go back to work, you will continue to receive your full benefits.

Miscellaneous Sources

During your retirement, certain personal investments can be adjusted to produce a regular stream of income. Although these sources are available at any time, it is probably wise to postpone tapping them until sometime later in life. Besides inflation, other unanticipated events can cause a need for additional income at any time.

Annuities and life insurance contain values that make them ideal sources for future income. The ability to postpone income taxation on the accumulations within these contracts provides an excellent vehicle for providing income later. After several years of retirement, the need for the death benefit of a life insurance policy could become less important to you,[8] which would make the cash surrender value in this insurance another prime candidate for later income.

The equity in your home is also an excellent source for retirement income. This can be accomplished by downsizing your residence. Sell your current home, take a tax exemption for up to $500,000 of capital gains for married couples ($250,000 for a single person), and buy a smaller, lower-priced residence. Or you may choose to remain in your current home but arrange for a reverse mortgage—a contract between you and a financial institution or individual who pays you a monthly income based on the value of your real estate. At your death, or some other agreed-upon date, this flow of money is repaid from the sale of your residence.

So there it is! Your retirement income will probably come from one or more of three sources: Social Security, employer retirement plans, and personal wealth accumulation. The third source is rapidly becoming the most important.

Retirement working, if you will allow that combination of words, might provide a part of your retirement income. The AARP has many publications on this subject that are available at very reasonable prices. Their phone number for information is 800-424-3410, and their Web address is *www.aarp.org*.

And you won't have to worry about being able to find employment if you choose to work. According to Watson Wyatt Worldwide, a consulting firm in Bethesda, Maryland, work demand will be great. "There will be an increasing demand for labor combined with a decline in the number of workers ages 24–45 in the next decade. This will create a 30 percent shortage of workers."

It is worth emphasizing again the importance of arriving at the retirement stage of life with sufficient assets to allow you to choose whether or not you work. Even when work is an acceptable choice, many future events may either force you to stop working or leave you with the poor choice of working under dire circumstances such as a disability, an undesirable job, family obligations, or no opportunities to be engaged in nonwork activities you long to pursue. Plan for money forever and keep control over the important choices you may have to make during this wonderful stage of your life.

By now our friends Paul and Paula Persons know more about the three sources of retirement income than do most people. The Persons really appreciated the excellent referral to their financial consultant, Tad Early. They feel very lucky that they were able to persuade Tad to take on one last client, especially since he had recently lived through many of the aspects of retirement planning himself.

notes

1. The Employee Retirement Income Security Act of 1974.

2. Replacement Ratio is a percentage of pre-retirement income. Replacement Ratio is determined by dividing the Social Security benefit by pre-retirement income. For example: $15,200 ÷ $80,000 = 19 percent. This example illustrates that a Social Security benefit of $15,200 is 19 percent of pre-retirement income ($80,000).

3. FICA, or Federal Insurance Contributions Act, calls for a payroll tax that is applied to the funding of Social Security and Medicare benefits.

4. 100 percent of $10,000 + 3.5 percent of $10,000 = $10,000 + $350 = $10,350.

5. For purposes of determining profitability, an employer lumps together salary plus benefits as a single expense. When a company's profits begin to decrease, the employer usually cuts expenses. Options that the employer has in regard to employees include terminating employees, decreasing salaries and benefits, decreasing only salaries, or decreasing only benefits. To an employee, these options are probably listed in order of increasing desirability if the employee has a choice of such undesirable choices.

6. Investments include federally insured savings accounts. In fact, as you will learn in Chapter 12, it is wise to always have a certain percentage of your investments in low-risk, highly liquid vehicles. You also will learn about other vehicles that are as safe as savings accounts and may pay greater interest.

7. Your income before any deductions are made for income tax, Social Security tax, and so forth.

8. Examples are policies purchased to protect children who now may be on their own, to guarantee the mortgage on a house that no longer has a mortgage, to provide education for children who long ago graduated, and so on.

the wobbly three-legged stool

chapter 8

Cashing In On Your Retirement Plans

Penelope and Percy Pennypincher worked hard all their lives to earn a living and raise a family. They also worked hard to save at least 10 percent of all their take-home pay. They even planned carefully with their advisors to invest these savings profitably.

As they approached retirement, all their children were emancipated—a legal term for "on their own"—and some were even starting their own families. So Percy was not surprised one night at the dinner table when Penelope said, "Let's retire and take a trip around the world."

Percy paused as if in deep thought and then replied, "Let's retire and go in and watch the game on television." After some more playful banter, they agreed retirement was the right choice. Their only problem was that they hadn't a clue what to do next.

All sorts of new questions popped into their minds. When and how should they begin to withdraw some or all of the money they had saved? Did they have choices, and if so, what were they? What would be the right choices for their situation?

Penelope and Percy were not the first people to reach this very important decision-making point in their lives, nor were they the last. Some of you already have passed this point, but you still have decisions to make on the best payout options to elect. Others, having already made these elections, might choose to skip to the section on annuity options later in this chapter. And still others might simply choose to read on for a better understanding of this very important information.

Those of you who have not reached the retirement decision stage but are rapidly approaching it must recognize that this is a point of no return—some of your decisions will be irreversible once made. Collect as much information as you can before you make any decisions. For example, you should know every plan's distribution options, the taxation ramifications of withdrawals, the future inflation adjustments, if any, and the amount of benefits both for you and for a surviving beneficiary. And all this is just a start.

This is get-serious time; allow as much time as possible. Even a year or two is not too much time. Most administrators of employer retirement plans will provide estimates prior to your actual retirement date. Financial consultants can project Social Security, employer pension plans, and personal wealth accumulation over your many retirement years to determine how solvent your retirement bank will be. When you do these projections, be sure to include our old enemy inflation in all calculations. Taxation will be discussed in Chapter 13, but remember that all decisions should be made only after you have considered the tax ramifications.

Now let's get down to some basics. You can elect to receive retirement money in only two fundamental ways: (1) *all at once*, or (2) *periodic payments*. Actually, it is sometimes possible to have the option of a combination of these two methods of distribution, which we will get to later.

All at once is usually called a lump sum or single sum distribution. For taxation purposes, *lump sum* has a specific definition in the Internal Revenue Code. All plans in which you have elected a reduction in wages to make contributions will allow for a lump sum distribution. Such plans include 401(k), 403(b), Simplified Employee Pension Plans (or SEPs), and Individual Retirement

Accounts (or IRAs). Some, but not all, employer retirement plans have as one of the options a lump sum distribution.

Periodic payments are available from most plans. These payments could be for a certain number of years, for the remainder of your life, or for your lifetime plus a beneficiary's lifetime, if longer than yours.

Among the first facts you want to collect are (1) what distribution options you have, and (2) how much money is involved for each. Keep in mind that if you have more than one plan you need to get all the facts for each plan.

Let's review a few hypothetical but representational case studies to help you understand various retirement plan options.

Option 1

Sally Solo is about to retire. Her husband died twenty years ago. His life insurance plus her full employment provided sufficient income to complete the rearing and educating of their two children. Both children are now married and have families of their own. One of Sally's children is a successful doctor; the other is a successful lawyer.

Sally never remarried. Even with all of her financial obligations, she was able to invest some of her income. She also has a company pension plan that will provide a very important part of her projected retirement income. Even with her investments, she still needs the maximum income from the pension plan that is available. So, after reviewing all the options, Sally selected lifetime monthly payments with no survivor benefit. This produces the maximum monthly dollar amount guaranteed for Sally's life and terminates upon her death.

Of course, Sally plans to live to be 100 years old, but whether she does or does not live that long, she believes the risk of not leaving a residual benefit for a beneficiary is not that important. Her children do not need the money as much as she needs the greatest amount possible guaranteed for life.

Option 2

Doris and Daryl Duo decided soon after marriage that they would not have children. They both worked full-time and now have decided to retire. Doris and Daryl worked for different companies, but their pension plans are quite similar in amounts and options.

The option that seemed best for them was lifetime monthly payments from each plan, and at the death of either Duo, 50 percent of the benefit will continue to the survivor for his or her lifetime. Naturally this would reduce the monthly amount. Think of it this way. Before the death of one Duo, two payments were coming to their home every month. After the death of one Duo, the surviving partner receives only one and one-half payments. The Duos consider this reduction to be small, and the survivor probably will need only a little more than what his or her own plan provides. Furthermore, Doris and Daryl feel that after all those years of work, to lose all at death, as in Option 1, would not be fair to the survivor.

Option 3

Fred and Freda Family raised twelve children during Fred's successful career as a pharmacist. He helped manage a small, high-quality pharmacy. The owner considered Fred to be a key person in his dual role of pharmacist and manager and established a very lucrative pension for him. Since Freda never worked outside the home, it was very important to Fred that his retirement income benefits be assigned to her at as high a level as possible. So Fred and Freda decided that the best option for them would be the same option as Option 2, except the benefit to the survivor would equal 100 percent of Fred's benefit. This causes the monthly benefit to be lower than in Option 1 or Option 2, but it provides larger benefits for the survivor than Option 2, and those benefits continue for the balance of the survivor's life.

Option 4

Gary and Gail Gap have a September-April marriage. Gary is 70 years old. Gail is 34. They have been married only three years and have two children. Gary is about to retire. He has been trying to retire for the past four years, but he is such a key person that his employer has been able to entice him to continue working. "But not this time," says Gary.

Gary and Gail have a difficult decision on the selection of the proper option in his pension plan. Option 1 is not even a consideration, because Gail would need income if Gary died before their children were raised. Choosing Options 2 or 3 would require a significant reduction in Gary's benefit because a survivor's benefit is based on the difference between the spouses' ages.

A reasonable compromise would be lifetime monthly payments for Gary, and a guarantee that these payments would continue to Gail if Gary died within a certain period of time. This option usually states that payments will be made to the participant for life with a minimum of a preselected period of time, such as ten, fifteen, or twenty years. If the participant does not live for this period of time, the payments would continue to a named beneficiary for the remainder of the selected period. Naturally, the longer the period guaranteed, the lower the payment. Gary feels that by selecting a twenty-year guarantee, the benefit would at least get their children raised.

Option 5

William Widower has elected to retire early at age 52. He was a schoolteacher in a private school and had no retirement plan until ten years ago. His pay was low, but because of income he receives from an inheritance, he was able to take a job of choice rather than one of necessity.

Ten years ago, he took an administrative position in the

local public schools that offered both a retirement plan and a tax-sheltered annuity plan, a 403(b). His much higher income during these ten years allowed for the maximum 403(b) salary reductions. His income from the inheritance continued through this period, but all payments are in constant dollars—that is, there is no provision for cost-of-living adjustments.

Thus the purchasing power of this income has been reduced significantly over these years by high rates of inflation, and it's likely to continue to diminish in the future. William calculated that by not touching the money accumulating in the 403(b) plan it would grow substantially over the next ten-year period. He concluded that the 403(b) plan combined with Social Security beginning at age 62 and income from his inheritance would be proper for a long retirement. However, he wants to retire now, at age 52, ten years before the 403(b) plan and Social Security would kick in.

William decides that his retirement plan from school can provide the needed income from age 52 to 62. He further decides that his best choice would be the option that provides for a monthly payment for a certain period—ten, fifteen, or twenty years. William selects a ten-year payout. The benefit will stop at the end of the selected period even if William is still living. But in his case, the end of the selected period is when his other assets, notably 403(b) and Social Security, could begin to pay out.[1] William thinks it is nothing less than a tailor-made solution for his situation.

Option 6

Lewis Lump retained the services of a financial consultant to discuss his retirement options. Lewis decided to receive his pension benefit in a single payment. Lewis participates in one of the growing number of plans that have this option. He now has another decision to make. He has to decide whether to accept this lump sum distribution and pay tax under ten-year averaging, for which he qualifies,[2] or to roll over these proceeds into an Individual Retirement Account (IRA). (See Chapter 13 for more information about rollovers.)

Part of the reason Lewis is selecting a lump sum distribution is that his pension plan does not offer inflation adjustments in its lifetime monthly payments option. This is true of the majority of plans. Lewis expects to have a long life. He also understands how inflation reduces the purchasing power of level lifetime payments. Therefore, Lewis will take his lump sum distribution and, with the advice of his financial consultant, invest the assets in ways that keep ahead of the ravages of inflation.

Lewis recognizes that assets in an IRA or a 403(b) plan have special withdrawal requirements. Also, the year a person becomes $70\frac{1}{2}$ years old, he (or she) must withdraw at least a certain amount from the retirement account(s) or be subject to a 50 percent tax penalty. (See Chapter 13 for details on Minimum Required Distribution.)

For example, consider the following case. Maude Linn is 70 years old and very ill. She is not expected to live another year. She has lived alone since she and her husband divorced many years ago. She got the children. Now she is about to retire. Her children—her beneficiaries—are adults now, but they are a long way from retirement. Maude's advisor tells her that a lump sum distribution rolled over into an IRA with her children as beneficiaries might maximize the benefit to them. This way, the moneys would become taxable only as the children receive them, and the payout period could be extended over many years. (See Chapter 13 for a thorough discussion of this very important matter.) Maude elects Option 6, a lump sum distribution that is rolled over into an IRA.

cashing in

Summary of Usual Options in Retirement Plans[3]

Option 1:
Lifetime Monthly Payments with no survivor benefits

> This option produces the largest lifetime monthly income.

Option 2:
Lifetime Monthly Payments with a lifetime payment of 50 percent to a surviving beneficiary

> There is a reduction in the participant's monthly benefit. Usually the reduction is small if the beneficiary's age is close to that of the participant.

Option 3:
Lifetime Monthly Payments with a lifetime payment of 100 percent to a surviving beneficiary

> This option is the same as Option 2 except that the surviving beneficiary would receive the same amount as the participant was receiving. Because this produces a much greater survivor benefit, the reduction in the participant's benefit is greater.

Option 4:
Lifetime Monthly Payments with a guarantee of a minimum number of years (no special surviving spousal benefit)

> The benefit is reduced according to the number of years payments are guaranteed.

Option 5:
Guaranteed Monthly Payments for a certain number of years

> Payments are not guaranteed for life but for a selected number of years—ten, fifteen, or twenty years, typically. Depending on the number of years selected, the payments could be greater than or less than Option 1.

Option 6:
Lump Sum

> All the assets in the participant's account are distributed in a single amount.

All the foregoing case studies have provided you with an informative survey of the major options that may be available to anyone who is about to retire. As you no doubt recognize, there are various combinations of options and even many options within options. This is why each person should consult with one or more experts before making important decisions that can affect the rest of his or her life. The examples provided here should make you more aware of the questions you should ask as you consult your advisor(s).

Annuities

Investors, such as yourself, frequently hear about the tax advantages of investing in annuities. Annuities are investment contracts distributed by most financial institutions. They offer a variety of investment vehicles—such as bonds, stocks, and real estate—in which you can invest your money. A main feature of annuities is your ability to postpone taxation until accumulated monies are withdrawn.

The government periodically considers changing the rules, but so far has not taken away the tax deferral on annuity accumulations. Under present law, all money in an annuity earns profits on which you can delay paying income tax. Since the tax is deferred (until you withdraw the funds from the annuity), you accumulate more to earn more.[4] It truly is an extraordinary vehicle for accumulating retirement money.

In years past, when the time came for a client to retire, many investment advisors did not recommend annuitizing—that is, changing the investment into an income stream for life. The major reason was a concern about a vehicle that produces only a level income for life while living expenses probably would increase. This was William Widower's concern in Option 5. The following graph shows why this concern is valid. In particular, compare the line that represents a level payout with the line that represents inflation. In 1972, the beginning of the comparison, the graph shows that $12,000 worth of goods and services cost

$12,000. On January 1, 2002, however, the graph shows that the same goods and services cost about $51,470.

Value of a $12,000 Initial Annual Payment

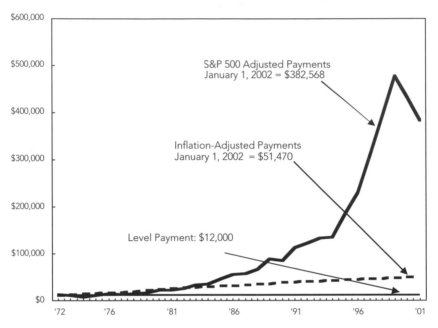

With an average annual rate of inflation of 5% from 1971 through 2001, a person on a level income (although guaranteed) has not fared very well.

Variable Annuities

Now suppose a person were offered the option to select a payout that is based on the Standard & Poor's 500 Index, which for the period from 1972 through 2001 produced an average annual return more than double that of inflation (the S&P Index averaged 12.2 percent, while inflation averaged 5 percent). The instrument that could provide similar results is the annuitization of a *variable annuity*.

The word *annuitization* may be new to some of you because this word is just beginning to be used frequently. The concept behind the word is what this chapter is all about. In retirement plans, annuitization is the same as the options previously discussed.

A *variable annuity* is a contract that has all the features of a regular annuity plus the option to invest the money in one or more stock portfolios. Many of these portfolios reflect, plus or minus a percentage point, the S&P 500. The insurance companies do have charges for managing the investments that reduce the total results. But such charges are small when compared to the historic rates of return of the stock market (variable annuity) versus the bond market (regular annuity).

The annuitization of a variable annuity has the potential advantage of a stream of payments that will increase as the underlying stock portfolio increases in value. It is important also to note that the payments will be both up and down as the stock portfolio increases and decreases in value. But with proper diversification in the remainder of your total investment portfolio, these fluctuations can be tolerated far more easily than can the diminishing purchasing power of a level or regular annuity.

The annuitization of a variable annuity is the ultimate vehicle to create money forever. The annuity payments continue as long as the annuitant or co-annuitant is alive. Other options provide for payments for a specific number of years to a beneficiary. The key is that the benefit continues regardless of how long the annuitant or annuitants live.

Another benefit of this annuitization is the application of the use of other people's money (OPM). This occurs from the way actuaries calculate the initial payout amount. The calculations are very complex, but the result is that the initial amount invested is assumed to be sufficient to pay out the benefit for the life of the annuitant. Since actuaries do not know the precise date any specific annuitant will die, they must assume a date, which is the end-date for the average life expectancy of a person the age and sex of the annuitant. It is a statistical guess.

If the annuitant continues to live beyond that date, there isn't any money left from the annuitant's investment to pay the benefits. In such cases, the reserves from other people's annuities who died before the actuarial-assumed date of death are used to continue benefit payments to those who live beyond their assumed date of death. This is benefiting from OPM, and it is hard to make more profits than through the use of OPM. All you have to do, of course, is live longer than what the actuaries expect the average person to live.

One caution: Don't put all your money into annuities. You know the common wisdom of not putting all your eggs in one basket. You should have many baskets of different kinds of assets. You will learn more about this in Chapters 10, 11, and 12.

Virtually every prospectus tells you that past performance is no guarantee of future performance. But look again at the graph. Which of the three lines would you have wanted to represent your income over this past thirty-year period?

§

Okay, you and your spouse are 70 years old. You have made all the right choices. You have $100,000 accumulated in an IRA, 401(k), or 403(b) plan. Until now, you have not had to take any money out of this plan. You have continued to receive the advantage of tax deferral while your investments have continued to grow. But you knew you'd have to pay taxes someday, didn't you? Well, you have reached the age when the IRS is knocking at your investment door. Since you will be $70\frac{1}{2}$ years old this year, the IRS requires you to start withdrawing money from your retirement account. They will wait no longer to begin to collect taxes on your investment.

It is important that you plan for these withdrawals and do not forget to make them. If you do not start withdrawing the money on time, the IRS will impose a 50 percent tax penalty on the amount you were required to withdraw but did not. A technicality in the law does allow you to postpone this first withdrawal until April 1 of the year after you reach age $70\frac{1}{2}$. If you do postpone this first withdrawal to the following year, however, you are required to make two withdrawals within that year.

Government tables dictate the minimum amount that you must withdraw each year. This amount is calculated by dividing the previous year-end value of your account by the factor shown in the table based on what your age will be at the end of the withdrawal year. For example, assume that the previous year-end value of your account is $100,000, and your age at the end of the current year (the withdrawal year) is 70. The factor for this age is 27.4. Therefore, $100,000 ÷ 27.4 = $3,649.64.

You probably are thinking the law can't be this simple. Well, you are right. There are situations in which the calculation would be different. For example, if the retiree has a spouse more than ten years younger, then the factor changes. Given the same information as before, except the spousal beneficiary is fifteen years younger, the factor is 31.1. Therefore, the calculation is: $100,000 ÷ 31.1 = $3,215.43. It is very important that you get expert advice when it is time to make this calculation. Not only can it be complicated, the tables can change from time to time, and because of the 50 percent penalty for underwithdrawing, it is imperative that at least the minimum required distribution be taken each year.[5]

notes

1. Keep in mind that 403(b) plans may be delayed beyond age 62, but it is William's desire to start withdrawals at age 62.

2. Born prior to January 1, 1937.

3. Some retirement plans offer more or fewer options and they may be numbered differently. Also, some plans offer Option 2 with various percentages either in place of 50 percent or in addition to it.

4. Money that normally would be paid annually to the government for taxes remains in the account to earn profits. The tax is deferred, or put off until later.

5. Note that we are talking about *minimum* amounts that are *required* to be withdrawn. You can always withdraw more than these minimums at any time. Of course, you pay tax on all withdrawals.

chapter 9

Making Your Money Last
a Lifetime

Sally and Sam Sensible are each 62 years old, and they want to retire. They were fortunate as well as bright when they were younger. They were fortunate to learn about the three sources of income and the importance of accumulating personal wealth to supplement their retirement plans and Social Security. (Discussed in Chapter 7.) They were bright enough to do something about it.

Sally and Sam also were fortunate to learn that they have choices to make when they retire and start to withdraw their retirement funds. (Presented in Chapter 8.) They were bright enough to consult with their advisors well before their retirement date and choose the best options for their circumstances.

The Sensibles also were fortunate to learn how to tell whether their money would last as long as they do after they retire. Do you know how to tell? The formula is very simple: Assets minus expenses plus profits equal how long your money will last. Sound like ninth-grade algebra? Well, there is a way to make it simpler than that.

If you do not have a computer, consider buying one. Yes, it presents another lifestyle adjustment that requires you to learn new skills. Yes, it is hard to make changes. Yes, you might be very accurate multiplying figures in your head or using pencil and paper or even using a calculator.

Nonetheless, it is time to take advantage of what the age of technology offers, especially if you need to make projections spanning at least thirty or forty years. There are many computations and variables involved, and when the results are not to your liking, you will want to change one or more of these factors. You will say, "What if I do this?" and "What if I change that?" Without a computer, it is simply too tedious and takes too long to play the necessary "what-if" games.

The computer program we created in our practice, the Retirement Cash Flow Analysis, makes it easy to calculate future retirement cash flow on a spreadsheet template.[1] This program can help you run through all the what-if scenarios you need or want in no time. My financial plan coordinator, Lori Gilbert, and my partner, Mark Davis, were of great assistance in the development and improvement of this program over several years. I feel comfortable in recommending it even if it requires you to begin a journey into the land of the computer.

My skepticism about any attempt to project into the future for more than two days grows stronger each year. Yet this financial tool has served my clients well for many years, and without some intelligent method to estimate your future cash-flow requirements, you will certainly guess wrong, perhaps with disastrous results. With this computer program at your disposal, at the very least you can rerun it periodically using actual history and more current assumptions, such as changes in the rate of inflation or returns on investments.

The amount of money that you decide you need annually in retirement has a profound effect on your ability to maintain an acceptable standard of living throughout this time period. This is especially true when your retirement years are many, as they should be. Remember: More and more people are living into their 90s and beyond. Naturally, you and I will be among them.

Let's revisit Sally and Sam Sensible as an example of how spending can affect one's future standard of living. Recall that they plan to retire at age 62. Let's consider their financial vital statistics shown below.

Investment Assets	$240,000
Level Pension (no inflation adjustment)	$24,000
Social Security	$21,750

Now it is time to make some assumptions—possibly the most critical being how long you will live. The most current information on longevity comes from the 2000 Annuity Mortality Table. It shows that if you live to age 65, your average life expectancy is age 87. Average here means that one-half of the 65-year-olds will still be alive at age 87. For a couple who live to age 65, the average life expectancy for at least one of the couple is age 93.

Annual Percentage of Deaths Starting at Age 65

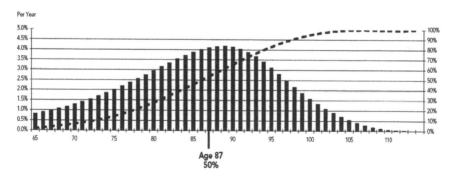

Source: 2000 Individual Annuity Mortality Table

making your money last

Percentage of 65-Year-Old Couples, At Least One of Whom Will Live to Various Ages

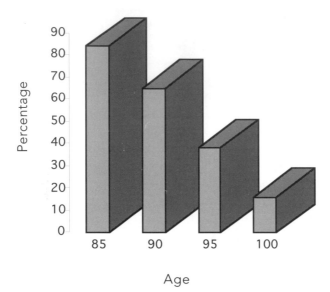

Source: 2000 Individual Annuity Mortality Table

Let's think positively. Let's say that Sally and Sam Sensible will live to be 100. Let's say that during this time, inflation will be 3 percent a year for ten years and 3.5 percent a year thereafter. Let's also assume that the total return on the Sensibles' investments will average 8 percent a year. We enter this into our computer program. Then we enter Sally and Sam's desired annual income. Taking advantage of the program's powers of computation, we go a step further and enter three different desired income amounts and, after entering each, run the program to see how this affects the results.

SALLY AND SAM SENSIBLE

RETIREMENT CASH FLOW ANALYSIS

SIGNIFICANT ASSUMPTIONS

1.	YEAR OF RETIREMENT				2002
2.	YEAR BORN:	RETIREE 1	SAM		1940
2A.		RETIREE 2	SALLY		1940

3.	ANNUAL INFLATION RATE FOR YEARS	1-10	3.0%	11-20	3.5%	THEREAFTER	3.5%
4.	SOCIAL SECURITY INFLATION RATE						3.0%
5.	AFTER-TAX RATE OF RETURN ON INVESTMENTS						8.0%
6.	PENSION INFLATION AJD:	OPT 1 = COMPOUNDED INFL RATE			0.0%	SAM	0.0% SALLY
6A.		OPT 2 = FLAT FIXED DOLLAR AMT			$0	SAM	$0 SALLY

RETIREMENT DOLLARS

7.	ANNUAL DESIRED INCOME (EXCLUDING MORTGAGE)				$45,000
8.	ANNUAL MORTGAGE PMT (PRIN & INT ONLY)	ENDING	0		$0
9.	SOCIAL SECURITY	SAM	STARTING	2002	$14,500
9A.		SALLY	STARTING	2002	$7,250
10.	CAPITAL AVAILABLE FOR INVESTING				$240,000
11.	PENSION BENEFITS	SAM	STARTING	2002	$24,000
11A.		SALLY	STARTING	0	$0
12.	ADDITIONAL ANNUAL INVESTMENTS NEEDED				$0

YEAR	AGE 1	AGE 2	REQUIRED INCOME	MORTGAGE PAYMENT	SOCIAL SECURITY	OTHER INC (EXPENSES)	PENSION SAM	PENSION SALLY	AMT NEEDED FROM CAPITAL	REMAINING CAPITAL	SHORTFALL
2002	62	62	45,000	0	21,750	0	24,000	0	(750)	259,980	0
2003	63	63	46,350	0	22,403	0	24,000	0	(52)	280,833	0
2004	64	64	47,741	0	23,075	0	24,000	0	666	302,607	0
2005	65	65	49,173	0	23,767	0	24,000	0	1,406	325,354	0
2006	66	66	50,648	0	24,480	0	24,000	0	2,168	349,127	0
2007	67	67	52,167	0	25,214	0	24,000	0	2,953	373,986	0
2008	68	68	53,732	0	25,971	0	24,000	0	3,762	399,993	0
2009	69	69	55,344	0	26,750	0	24,000	0	4,595	427,214	0
2010	70	70	57,005	0	27,552	0	24,000	0	5,452	455,720	0
2011	71	71	58,715	0	28,379	0	24,000	0	6,336	485,588	0
2012	72	72	60,476	0	29,230	0	24,000	0	7,246	516,900	0
2013	73	73	62,593	0	30,107	0	24,000	0	8,486	549,426	0
2014	74	74	64,784	0	31,010	0	24,000	0	9,773	583,216	0
2015	75	75	67,051	0	31,941	0	24,000	0	11,110	618,319	0
2016	76	76	69,398	0	32,899	0	24,000	0	12,499	654,785	0
2017	77	77	71,827	0	33,886	0	24,000	0	13,941	692,669	0
2018	78	78	74,341	0	34,902	0	24,000	0	15,438	732,027	0
2019	79	79	76,943	0	35,949	0	24,000	0	16,993	772,916	0
2020	80	80	79,636	0	37,028	0	24,000	0	18,608	815,397	0
2021	81	81	82,423	0	38,139	0	24,000	0	20,204	859,533	0
2022	82	82	85,308	0	39,283	0	24,000	0	22,025	905,390	0
2023	83	83	88,293	0	40,461	0	24,000	0	23,832	953,036	0
2024	84	84	91,384	0	41,675	0	24,000	0	25,708	1,002,542	0
2025	85	85	94,582	0	42,926	0	24,000	0	27,657	1,053,983	0
2026	86	86	97,893	0	44,213	0	24,000	0	29,679	1,107,435	0
2027	87	87	101,319	0	45,540	0	24,000	0	31,779	1,162,979	0
2028	88	88	104,865	0	46,906	0	24,000	0	33,959	1,220,700	0
2029	89	89	108,535	0	48,313	0	24,000	0	36,222	1,280,685	0
2030	90	90	112,334	0	49,762	0	24,000	0	38,572	1,343,026	0
2031	91	91	116,266	0	51,255	0	24,000	0	41,010	1,407,817	0
2032	92	92	120,335	0	52,793	0	24,000	0	43,542	1,475,159	0
2033	93	93	124,547	0	54,377	0	24,000	0	46,170	1,545,155	0
2034	94	94	128,906	0	56,008	0	24,000	0	48,898	1,617,913	0
2035	95	95	133,418	0	57,688	0	24,000	0	51,729	1,693,548	0
2036	96	96	138,087	0	59,419	0	24,000	0	54,668	1,772,177	0
2037	97	97	142,920	0	61,202	0	24,000	0	57,719	1,853,924	0
2038	98	98	147,922	0	63,038	0	24,000	0	60,885	1,938,918	0
2039	99	99	153,100	0	64,929	0	24,000	0	64,171	2,027,293	0
2040	100	100	158,458	0	66,877	0	24,000	0	67,582	2,119,192	0

THIS ANALYSIS IS BASED ON THE ACCURACY AND CONSISTENCY OF THE DATA AND ASSUMPTIONS YOU HAVE PROVIDED IN ITEMS 1 THROUGH 11 AND IS NOT GUARANTEED. THE FIGURES SHOWN ARE VALID ONLY AS LONG AS THE DATA AND ASSUMPTIONS REMAIN UNCHANGED. TO MAINTAIN ACCURACY OF THIS ANALYSIS, PERIODIC UPDATING IS NECESSARY TO REFLECT CHANGES AS THEY OCCUR.

making your money last

SALLY AND SAM SENSIBLE

RETIREMENT CASH FLOW ANALYSIS

SIGNIFICANT ASSUMPTIONS

1.	YEAR OF RETIREMENT						2002
2.	YEAR BORN:	RETIREE 1		SAM			1940
2A.		RETIREE 2		SALLY			1940
3.	ANNUAL INFLATION RATE FOR YEARS	1-10	3.0%	11-20	3.5%	THEREAFTER	3.5%
4.	SOCIAL SECURITY INFLATION RATE						3.0%
5.	AFTER-TAX RATE OF RETURN ON INVESTMENTS						8.0%
6.	PENSION INFLATION AJD:	OPT 1 = COMPOUNDED INFL RATE			0.0%	SAM	0.0% SALLY
6A.		OPT 2 = FLAT FIXED DOLLAR AMT			$0	SAM	$0 SALLY

					RETIREMENT DOLLARS
7.	ANNUAL DESIRED INCOME (EXCLUDING MORTGAGE)				$51,000
8.	ANNUAL MORTGAGE PMT (PRIN & INT ONLY)	ENDING	0		$0
9.	SOCIAL SECURITY	SAM	STARTING	2002	$14,500
9A.		SALLY	STARTING	2002	$7,250
10.	CAPITAL AVAILABLE FOR INVESTING				$240,000
11.	PENSION BENEFITS	SAM	STARTING	2002	$24,000
11A.		SALLY	STARTING	0	$0
12.	ADDITIONAL ANNUAL INVESTMENTS NEEDED				$0

YEAR	AGE 1	AGE 2	REQUIRED INCOME	MORTGAGE PAYMENT	SOCIAL SECURITY	OTHER INC (EXPENSES)	PENSION SAM	PENSION SALLY	AMT NEEDED FROM CAPITAL	REMAINING CAPITAL	SHORTFALL
2002	62	62	51,000	0	21,750	0	24,000	0	5,250	253,740	0
2003	63	63	52,530	0	22,403	0	24,000	0	6,128	267,667	0
2004	64	64	54,106	0	23,075	0	24,000	0	7,031	281,767	0
2005	65	65	55,729	0	23,767	0	24,000	0	7,962	296,028	0
2006	66	66	57,401	0	24,480	0	24,000	0	8,921	310,432	0
2007	67	67	59,123	0	25,214	0	24,000	0	9,909	324,962	0
2008	68	68	60,897	0	25,971	0	24,000	0	10,926	339,596	0
2009	69	69	62,724	0	26,750	0	24,000	0	11,974	354,310	0
2010	70	70	64,605	0	27,552	0	24,000	0	13,053	369,080	0
2011	71	71	66,543	0	28,379	0	24,000	0	14,165	383,875	0
2012	72	72	68,540	0	29,230	0	24,000	0	15,310	398,663	0
2013	73	73	70,939	0	30,107	0	24,000	0	16,832	413,052	0
2014	74	74	73,421	0	31,010	0	24,000	0	18,411	426,948	0
2015	75	75	75,991	0	31,941	0	24,000	0	20,051	440,251	0
2016	76	76	78,651	0	32,899	0	24,000	0	21,752	452,849	0
2017	77	77	81,404	0	33,886	0	24,000	0	23,518	464,619	0
2018	78	78	84,253	0	34,902	0	24,000	0	25,350	475,424	0
2019	79	79	87,202	0	35,949	0	24,000	0	27,252	485,115	0
2020	80	80	90,254	0	37,028	0	24,000	0	29,226	493,530	0
2021	81	81	93,413	0	38,139	0	24,000	0	31,274	500,487	0
2022	82	82	96,682	0	39,283	0	24,000	0	33,399	505,791	0
2023	83	83	100,066	0	40,461	0	24,000	0	35,605	509,226	0
2024	84	84	103,568	0	41,675	0	24,000	0	37,893	510,555	0
2025	85	85	107,193	0	42,926	0	24,000	0	40,268	509,521	0
2026	86	86	110,945	0	44,213	0	24,000	0	42,732	505,842	0
2027	87	87	114,828	0	45,540	0	24,000	0	45,288	499,209	0
2028	88	88	118,847	0	46,906	0	24,000	0	47,941	489,287	0
2029	89	89	123,007	0	48,313	0	24,000	0	50,694	475,709	0
2030	90	90	127,312	0	49,762	0	24,000	0	53,549	458,074	0
2031	91	91	131,768	0	51,255	0	24,000	0	56,512	435,947	0
2032	92	92	136,380	0	52,793	0	24,000	0	59,587	408,853	0
2033	93	93	141,153	0	54,377	0	24,000	0	62,776	376,274	0
2034	94	94	146,093	0	56,008	0	24,000	0	66,085	337,647	0
2035	95	95	151,207	0	57,688	0	24,000	0	69,518	292,360	0
2036	96	96	156,499	0	59,419	0	24,000	0	73,080	239,746	0
2037	97	97	161,976	0	61,202	0	24,000	0	76,775	179,080	0
2038	98	98	167,645	0	63,038	0	24,000	0	80,608	109,575	0
2039	99	99	173,513	0	64,929	0	24,000	0	84,584	30,373	0
2040	100	100	179,586	0	66,877	0	24,000	0	31,588	0	57,122

THIS ANALYSIS IS BASED ON THE ACCURACY AND CONSISTENCY OF THE DATA AND ASSUMPTIONS YOU HAVE PROVIDED IN ITEMS 1 THROUGH 11 AND IS NOT GUARANTEED. THE FIGURES SHOWN ARE VALID ONLY AS LONG AS THE DATA AND ASSUMPTIONS REMAIN UNCHANGED. TO MAINTAIN ACCURACY OF THIS ANALYSIS, PERIODIC UPDATING IS NECESSARY TO REFLECT CHANGES AS THEY OCCUR.

SALLY AND SAM SENSIBLE
RETIREMENT CASH FLOW ANALYSIS

SIGNIFICANT ASSUMPTIONS

1.	YEAR OF RETIREMENT			2002
2.	YEAR BORN:	RETIREE 1	SAM	1940
2A.		RETIREE 2	SALLY	1940

3.	ANNUAL INFLATION RATE FOR YEARS	1-10	3.0%	11-20	3.5%	THEREAFTER	3.5%
4.	SOCIAL SECURITY INFLATION RATE						3.0%
5.	AFTER-TAX RATE OF RETURN ON INVESTMENTS						8.0%
6.	PENSION INFLATION AJD:	OPT 1 = COMPOUNDED INFL RATE			0.0%	SAM	0.0% SALLY
6A.		OPT 2 = FLAT FIXED DOLLAR AMT			$0	SAM	$0 SALLY

					RETIREMENT DOLLARS
7.	ANNUAL DESIRED INCOME (EXCLUDING MORTGAGE)				$55,500
8.	ANNUAL MORTGAGE PMT (PRIN & INT ONLY)	ENDING	0		$0
9.	SOCIAL SECURITY	SAM	STARTING	2002	$14,500
9A.		SALLY	STARTING	2002	$7,250
10.	CAPITAL AVAILABLE FOR INVESTING				$240,000
11.	PENSION BENEFITS	SAM	STARTING	2002	$24,000
11A.		SALLY	STARTING	0	$0
12.	ADDITIONAL ANNUAL INVESTMENTS NEEDED				$0

YEAR	AGE 1	AGE 2	REQUIRED INCOME	MORTGAGE PAYMENT	SOCIAL SECURITY	OTHER INC (EXPENSES)	PENSION SAM	PENSION SALLY	AMT NEEDED FROM CAPITAL	REMAINING CAPITAL	SHORTFALL
2002	62	62	55,500	0	21,750	0	24,000	0	9,750	249,060	0
2003	63	63	57,165	0	22,403	0	24,000	0	10,763	257,792	0
2004	64	64	58,880	0	23,075	0	24,000	0	11,805	266,138	0
2005	65	65	60,646	0	23,767	0	24,000	0	12,880	274,034	0
2006	66	66	62,466	0	24,480	0	24,000	0	13,986	281,411	0
2007	67	67	64,340	0	25,214	0	24,000	0	15,126	288,194	0
2008	68	68	66,270	0	25,971	0	24,000	0	16,299	294,298	0
2009	69	69	68,258	0	26,750	0	24,000	0	17,508	299,633	0
2010	70	70	70,306	0	27,552	0	24,000	0	18,753	304,100	0
2011	71	71	72,415	0	28,379	0	24,000	0	20,036	307,591	0
2012	72	72	74,587	0	29,230	0	24,000	0	21,357	309,986	0
2013	73	73	77,198	0	30,107	0	24,000	0	23,091	310,771	0
2014	74	74	79,900	0	31,010	0	24,000	0	24,890	309,747	0
2015	75	75	82,696	0	31,941	0	24,000	0	26,756	306,701	0
2016	76	76	85,591	0	32,899	0	24,000	0	28,692	301,398	0
2017	77	77	88,586	0	33,886	0	24,000	0	30,701	293,581	0
2018	78	78	91,687	0	34,902	0	24,000	0	32,785	282,971	0
2019	79	79	94,896	0	35,949	0	24,000	0	34,947	269,265	0
2020	80	80	98,217	0	37,028	0	24,000	0	37,189	252,129	0
2021	81	81	101,655	0	38,139	0	24,000	0	39,516	231,202	0
2022	82	82	105,213	0	39,283	0	24,000	0	41,930	206,092	0
2023	83	83	108,895	0	40,461	0	24,000	0	44,434	176,368	0
2024	84	84	112,707	0	41,675	0	24,000	0	47,031	141,564	0
2025	85	85	116,651	0	42,926	0	24,000	0	49,726	101,175	0
2026	86	86	120,734	0	44,213	0	24,000	0	52,521	54,647	0
2027	87	87	124,960	0	45,540	0	24,000	0	55,420	1,382	0
2028	88	88	129,333	0	46,906	0	24,000	0	1,437	0	56,991
2029	89	89	133,860	0	48,313	0	24,000	0	0	0	61,547
2030	90	90	138,545	0	49,762	0	24,000	0	0	0	64,783
2031	91	91	143,394	0	51,255	0	24,000	0	0	0	68,139
2032	92	92	148,413	0	52,793	0	24,000	0	0	0	71,620
2033	93	93	153,608	0	54,377	0	24,000	0	0	0	75,231
2034	94	94	158,984	0	56,008	0	24,000	0	0	0	78,976
2035	95	95	164,548	0	57,688	0	24,000	0	0	0	82,860
2036	96	96	170,307	0	59,419	0	24,000	0	0	0	86,889
2037	97	97	176,268	0	61,202	0	24,000	0	0	0	91,067
2038	98	98	182,438	0	63,038	0	24,000	0	0	0	95,400
2039	99	99	188,823	0	64,929	0	24,000	0	0	0	99,894
2040	100	100	195,432	0	66,877	0	24,000	0	0	0	104,555

THIS ANALYSIS IS BASED ON THE ACCURACY AND CONSISTENCY OF THE DATA AND ASSUMPTIONS YOU HAVE PROVIDED IN ITEMS 1 THROUGH 11 AND IS NOT GUARANTEED. THE FIGURES SHOWN ARE VALID ONLY AS LONG AS THE DATA AND ASSUMPTIONS REMAIN UNCHANGED. TO MAINTAIN ACCURACY OF THIS ANALYSIS, PERIODIC UPDATING IS NECESSARY TO REFLECT CHANGES AS THEY OCCUR.

making your money last

The table below summarizes the results of the three runs of the program.

Desired Annual Income	Value of Investment Assets at Age 100
$45,000	$2,119,192
$51,000	0
$55,500	0 at age 88

Look at the difference a few thousand dollars can make. If the Sensibles can live on $45,000[2] the first year, they can leave their heirs a rather nice legacy. If they decide to start retirement with $51,000 of income the first year, they can live without worry to the age of 100. The heirs receive nothing except the Sensibles' residence and personal property and life insurance. On the other hand, if Sally and Sam decide to live on $55,000 the first year, they will run out of money when they both reach the tender age of 88. From this side of 88, where they are now, this doesn't seem so bad. But suppose one or both of them live to be 89! Then what?

Perhaps, while on vacation, you have seen those bumper stickers that say, "We are spending our children's inheritance." These sticker owners should be aware that, without careful planning, they might last longer than their money and wind up on their children's doorstep.

There is no need to panic. Go back and review the figures for Sally and Sam Sensible. The differences are only a few thousand dollars a year plus inflation adjustments after the first year. With a reasonable amount of caution and careful planning at the outset, they should have no problems. Neither should you have any problems because now you can project what you want and what you will need to get it. If you don't like the first projection, you can make adjustments in one or more categories and make another projection. By running different projections now, you might have time to make the necessary adjustments that will bring your retirement dreams to fruition.

notes

1. To purchase this computer program, complete and mail the coupon included with this book, or write to: Haas Financial Services, Inc., 29600 Northwestern, #114, Southfield, MI 48034.

2. This amount is increased each year according to the assumption made about inflation. In other words, the standard of living will remain the same throughout the period discussed although the cost of living will not.

chapter 10

The Adventures of Jamie and Grandpa, Part 1: Two Types of Investments

Recent studies reveal that the number of adults who are intent on teaching sound financial habits to their offspring is greater today than at any other time in modern history. For these adults I offer the content of Chapters 10, 11, 12, and 16 as a possible introductory curriculum for instructing your children and grandchildren. For other readers with or without children, I offer these chapters as a review and extension of what knowledge you may already have. Suffice it to say, the adventures of Jamie and Grandpa are based on true experiences and should be read by everybody intent on making their money last forever.

"Grandpa, can we talk seriously?" The young voice interrupted the reverie that the senior citizen had just begun to enjoy.

"Sure, Jamie," Grandpa said. "What do you have in mind?"

"Well," Jamie said hesitantly, "what I would like to know is, Grandpa, are you rich?"

"We're all rich," Grandpa said, "if we have clean air to fill our lungs, bright sunshine to warm our bones, good friends to cheer our hearts . . . "

"Come on," Jamie interrupted. "You said we could talk seriously. I want to talk about money."

Grandpa didn't comment, so Jamie rushed on. "You seem to have everything you want. You travel all the time. You always bring me presents, and you never complain, like Mom and Dad, about not having enough money. So, you must be rich. Are you?"

Grandpa wondered why a sixteen-year-old would be interested in such serious matters. He waited for Jamie to continue. "The other day I heard Mom and Dad talking about how financially secure you are, and they don't have to worry about ever having to take care of you. They mentioned an investment portfolio you developed over your lifetime. They said it was sufficient to take care of you forever. Grandpa, what's an investment portfolio?"

Grandpa stroked a beard that he didn't have, just for effect, stared intently at Jamie, and said, "Now, why would a young person like you be interested in something like an investment portfolio?"

"Because every time I ask when I should start something, you always tell me that I can't start any younger. So, I want to start an investment portfolio—whatever it is—so I can be rich like you when I grow older."

"Perhaps some people would call me rich," Grandpa said, "but I don't think of myself that way. Rich to me is having more money than you know what to do with. I'm not that rich. But if you think rich is having enough money to provide for my needs no matter how long I live, then I am rich."

"That's great, Grandpa," Jamie said, "but how did you get rich and what did an investment portfolio have to do with it?"

"Oh yes, my wealth and my investment portfolio," said Grandpa. "Jamie, I believe this is going to take more than one session. Before we begin, you must make an agreement with me."

"What's that?" asked Jamie.

"You must stop me whenever you don't understand something or when you've had enough. Okay?" Jamie nodded assent.

"Let's start with a basic of investing," Grandpa began. "Repeat after me: There are only two kinds of investments."

"Stop clowning, Grandpa," Jamie protested, "I can name lots of different investments that I've heard you talk about—stocks, bonds, annuities, real estate, gold, silver, and even diamonds."

"Good," Grandpa said proudly. "But all that you mentioned, as well as others you didn't, fall into two categories. When you invest your money, you do so either with an ownership interest or as a lender. There are important risk-reward differences between the two, and your goals should dictate the amount you invest as an owner and as a lender."

Jamie's hand was raised as a traffic cop would indicate a stop.

"Give me a simple example of each kind," Jamie said, and then quickly added, "please."

"An example of an ownership interest is your Mom and Dad's home. They made a down payment to acquire this owner-ship interest and now make monthly payments to pay off the mortgage so that, at a time in the future, they will be the sole owners."

"And an example of a lender investment?" Jamie prodded.

"Those U.S. savings bonds you bought with the money you earned last summer," Grandpa said. "You lent your money to the government, and after a period of time, the government will return it to you with interest."

"What about the risk-reward differences between the two that you mentioned?" asked Jamie. "In fact, what is a risk-reward?"

"Whenever you invest your money," Grandpa explained,

"you should know that you might lose some or all of it. That's the risk. You invest the money in order to get more money back. That's the reward. You need to understand the risks and rewards of each type of investment—owner or lender—in order to properly allocate your assets."

Jamie nodded, and Grandpa continued.

"When you own something, you run the risk that what you own could be destroyed partially or entirely. Let's use your parents' home as an example. It could be razed in part or in whole by fire. This is a tremendous risk, but it is controllable with care, firefighter assistance, and the transfer of the risk in dollars via insurance.

"Another kind of risk is a loss in value of what you own. In 1993 some homes in southern California were sold for much less than the purchase price of only a few years earlier because of a lack of demand. There was a story in the paper about the lady who had to sell her home for less than the balance on her mortgage. That meant she had to pay maybe thousands of dollars just to get out of ownership.

"A dozen or more years ago, homeowners on Love Canal found that discarded chemicals leached into the ground under their homes and caused people to become ill and even die. Their ownership became worthless.

"In both examples, there was no insurance available that would cover the loss.

"On the other hand, in most parts of the world, ownership of real estate has provided significant appreciation on the investment—a significant reward. When you own something that appreciates in value, those profits are yours. Even if you own only a part, that percentage of the appreciation, or profits, also is yours."

"Is it less risky and more rewarding just to lend money?" Jamie asked.

"It all depends," Grandpa said with a smile. "When you

lend money you usually receive a pledge of the return of your money on a specific date plus interest payable at an agreed-upon rate. Your reward is the amount of interest paid on the loan."

"That sounds much safer," Jamie said. "Less risky."

"The risk is that the borrower may become unable to pay the interest," Grandpa went on to explain, "if, say, the borrower became bankrupt. If this happens, you lose some if not all of your money."

Grandpa let Jamie digest this new thought before he continued.

"A much larger risk as a lender is the inflation risk. Suppose you invest in a bond issued by a major corporation such as Microsoft, IBM, Sears, or General Motors. Or you lend money to the U.S. government by purchasing a twenty-year U.S. government bond. Chances are that these companies and the government will be around in twenty years and you'll get back all the money you lent them, plus interest.

"But twenty years from now, the dollars you paid them are not likely to buy the same amount of goods and services they did twenty years earlier. Why? Because inflation will have diminished the value of your dollars."

Grandpa looked to see if Jamie understood all this. Jamie neither raised a hand to stop Grandpa nor gave a signal for him to go on. Grandpa went on anyway.

"Let me put it this way. Suppose the rate of inflation averages 4 percent each year. This means that what you could buy for a dollar at the beginning of the year would cost you a dollar and four cents to buy at the end of the year. You lost four cents in the purchasing power of your dollar."

Jamie nodded. Grandpa continued.

"At this rate, after eighteen years, your dollars would purchase only half as much as they do now.

"Look at this," Grandpa said as he retrieved a paper from his desk and handed it to Jamie. "This is a graph of how a thousand dollars loses purchasing power over a twenty-year period at annual inflation rates of 3.1 percent and 4 percent."

Inflation-Adjusted Purchasing Power

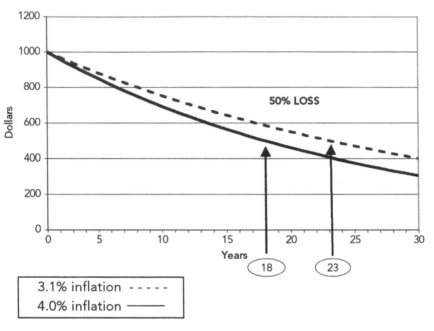

3.1% inflation - - - - -
4.0% inflation ———

At 3.1% inflation you would experience a 50% loss of your money in twenty-three years, and at 4 % inflation you would lose 50% of your money in just eighteen years.

"Grandpa," said Jamie, "I'm not sure I understand all of this, but I do recognize the application of what I just learned in my math class. It's called the Rule of 72. It helps you find out how long it takes for an interest rate to double an amount of money.[1] What you are talking about is like the Rule of 72 in reverse, where it shows how long it takes to cut the value in half."

"Exactly," said Grandpa. "The Rule of 72 in reverse. Instead of finding out how many years it takes an interest rate to double the value of something, it can be applied in reverse to show how many years it takes for inflation to cut purchasing power in half. I'll have to remember that."

Grandpa jotted a note to himself.

"Let's explore the loss of purchasing power due to inflation and why that is the key reason lending should be limited—very limited. When you lend money, you usually earn a fixed percent of the principle. If inflation continues year after year, this fixed interest has less value each year. The entire world has experienced inflation to one degree or another for some time now, and that's not likely to change. Under continued inflation, the loss of purchasing power is an insidious destroyer of wealth."

"Insidious?" Jamie interrupted.

"Yes, insidious," replied Grandpa. "Many people are not aware of how inflation eats away at their wealth. When you invest in ownership, the value of what you own usually keeps pace with inflation. When you invest as a lender, the value is constant and often falls behind inflation."

"Then why do people become lenders?" asked Jamie. "I thought buying U.S. government bonds, for example, is a low- or no-risk investment."

"It is, in one way. But people have been beguiled by the notion that buying U.S. government bonds is safer because there is less risk of losing the invested dollars, while earning interest at the same time," replied Grandpa. "Hidden in the shadows of time is the specter of inflation, which erodes the value of these dollars. Few people consider that risk."

"How would you do that, Grandpa?" asked Jamie.

"There can be more than one way to evaluate the risk," Grandpa answered. "Although no one can predict the future with certainty, history offers valuable signposts."

Jamie broke in. "So history shows that if inflation has averaged 4 percent a year for some years, I would be taking a big risk to buy a bond that pays only 3 percent a year. But my risk would be less if I could buy a bond that pays 8 percent a year."

"Very good," said a beaming Grandpa.

"I know that the purpose of sound investing is to get the best return for your money," Jamie said. "How do you compare investments to find the best one?"

"Hold the phone, Jamie. You just shifted gears without using the clutch!"

"What?" Jamie asked.

"Oh, I'm sorry," said Grandpa. "I slipped into my old lingo. Your question is a good one, so let's find an answer.

"To compare investments accurately," Grandpa continued, "you must always determine the total return of each investment over the same period of time."

"What is total return?" Jamie asked. "Isn't that the total amount of interest or dividends that you earn?"

"No," replied Grandpa, "total return is the change in the price of the bonds or stocks plus the amount of dividends or interest received. To show you what I mean about comparing total returns, let's pretend that we can hear the conversation among three friends. Their names are Hugh, Carol, and Gail. Each thinks that his or her investment is the most profitable compared to the other choices. Hugh starts the conversation."

Grandpa changes his voice to create the different parts.

Hugh: 'I invest in utility stocks because of their high dividend payout and stability.'

Carol: 'Not me. I stick to CDs. Sure, I get a little less payout in interest than your utility dividends, but I've got government insurance on my principal.'

Gail says: 'Well, maybe I'm a risk taker, but I choose common stocks of growth companies, and my current earnings are higher than either of yours.'

Hugh: 'But Gail, you only receive half the return of my utility stocks. That doesn't make sense to me.'

Carol: 'Even my CDs pay more than just about all

growth common stocks, and I understand some growth common stocks pay out nothing.'

Gail: 'But you have to include the increase in value of my stock when you compare returns on investments.'

"Both Hugh and Carol are looking at the return on their investment in terms of yield only.[2] Gail has gone one step further and combined dividends and the change in the price of the stock to determine profitability of her investment.

"Suppose Gail's stock was bought for ten dollars per share. After one year, the stock is selling for ten dollars and eighty-five cents per share. During that year, it paid a twenty-cent dividend. Now this dividend is only a 2 percent return on the ten-dollars-per-share investment.[3] But the total return is the price appreciation of eighty-five cents plus the dividend of twenty cents for a total return of one dollar and five cents. This is a total return of 10.5 percent.[4]

"By looking at both yield and appreciation, we learn the true return of an investment," Grandpa concludes. "Always look at the total return as the benchmark for comparison."

Jamie spoke quickly. "Maybe I'm shifting gears without using the clutch again, Grandpa, but has the stock market always been a good place to invest? In history class we learned about 1929, when the stock market crashed and investors were jumping out windows."

"Not all that many investors jumped out windows," said Grandpa, "although I suppose even one investor jumping out is one too many."

"Were there other bad times?" Jamie asked.

"Well, the 1930s weren't all that great for the stock market," answered Grandpa, "and 1957 and 1974 weren't so good either. Then there was the crash of 1987."

"It's beginning to sound like the stock market isn't a very good place at all," said Jamie.

"True, there have been some bad times to have money in the stock market," Grandpa replied. "But only if you choose to look at parts of the picture."

Grandpa opened the file drawer in his desk, took out a piece of paper, and showed it to Jamie. "For example, let's just look at the twenty-two years listed here. All of them were losers."

Negative Return Years for the Standard & Poor's 500

Year	Total Return	Year	Total Return	Year	Total Return
1929	-8.4	1941	-11.6	1973	-14.3
1930	-24.9	1946	-8.1	1974	-26.5
1931	-43.3	1953	-1.0	1977	-7.2
1932	-8.2	1957	-10.8	1981	-4.9
1934	-1.4	1962	-8.7	1990	-3.2
1937	-35.0	1966	-10.1	2000	-9.1
1939	-0.4	1969	-8.5	2001	-11.9
1940	-9.8				

"Bad times to invest," Jamie said after studying the chart.

Grandpa agreed and continued. "Let's suppose you invested one thousand dollars in the stock market at the beginning of each of those twenty-two terrible years and kept the money in the market until the end of year 2001. Here's a table that shows you how much each thousand would have earned and how much the total twenty-two thousand dollars would have earned."

Grandpa handed Jamie a piece of paper with the figures on it. "The table also shows a comparison with a similar investment in long-term U.S. government bonds."

$1,000 Invested in Each of the Stock Market's 22 Off Years

Year $1,000 Was Invested	S&P 500 Index		Long-Term Government Bonds	
	Value of Each $1,000 on 12/31/01	Average Rate of Return	Value of Each $1,000 on 12/31/01	Average Rate of Return
1929	$1,032,638	10.0%	$43,233	5.3%
1930	$1,127,334	10.3%	$41,812	5.3%
1931	$1,501,111	10.9%	$39,935	5.3%
1932	$2,647,462	11.9%	$42,170	5.5%
1934	$1,872,692	11.7%	$36,140	5.4%
1937	$960,347	11.1%	$29,107	5.3%
1939	$1,126,970	11.8%	$27,535	5.4%
1940	$1,131,496	12.0%	$26,001	5.4%
1941	$1,254,430	12.4%	$24,506	5.4%
1946	$573,366	12.0%	$20,255	5.5%
1953	$244,362	11.9%	$19,436	6.2%
1957	$115,300	11.1%	$18,783	6.7%
1962	$63,106	10.9%	$16,570	7.3%
1966	$42,946	11.0%	$14,696	7.8%
1969	$34,676	11.3%	$15,655	8.7%
1973	$26,790	12.0%	$12,298	9.0%
1974	$31,407	13.1%	$12,435	9.4%
1977	$25,158	13.8%	$9,339	9.3%
1981	$16,223	14.2%	$10,025	11.6%
1990	$4,263	12.8%	$2,930	9.4%
2000	$801	-10.5%	$1,260	12.2%
2001	$881	-11.9%	$1,037	3.7%
TOTAL	$13,833,759		$465,158	

two types of investments

Grandpa explained. "The table shows that if you had left each year's one thousand dollars in the stock market, even though you lost money each year you invested it, eventually you would have seen a positive return on your investments of well over thirteen million dollars. You also would have made nearly half a million dollars by investing in government bonds in each of these years, but the stock market was by far the better place to invest your twenty-two thousand dollars."

"The stock market looks like a sure place to invest money," said Jamie.

"Not at all," replied Grandpa. "First, the table shows history. It is no guarantee of what might happen in the future. Still, it would be very foolish to ignore what has happened in the past.

"Second," continued Grandpa, "how you buy stocks can make a difference. The table uses the Standard & Poor's 500 Index, also called the S&P 500, as a benchmark. You could have done better or worse depending on whether you had picked winning or losing stocks. So far, no one has been able to consistently pick only winning stocks."

"Then why shouldn't you just buy some S&P 500 stocks?" asked Jamie.

"The stocks in some companies," Grandpa replied, "used in the S&P 500 may be going down in value at the same time the stocks in other companies are going up. You would have to buy stock in all 500 companies, and there are very few people who can afford to do that. An S&P 500 Index mutual fund, however, would have closely reflected the results shown in the table."

"I know what a mutual fund[5] is, because you told me." Jamie said. "But what is an index mutual fund?"

"An index mutual fund is one that invests in a portfolio of stocks that replicates the whole stock market," Grandpa answered. "It doesn't own an equal number of shares of each and every company on all stock exchanges, but its portfolio is so broad that its ups and downs are very similar to the whole population of stocks. But remember, there are two types of investment."

"Yes, owning and lending," replied Jamie, "and I'm about convinced that ownership is better."

"There's an old saying that goes, 'Neither a borrower nor a lender be,'" said Grandpa, "but another old saying goes, 'Don't put all your eggs in one basket.' I would suggest that some of your money should be in each of these two kinds of investments, with the greater portion going into ownership. In another session we'll discuss how much of each type you should have in your investment portfolio. [See Chapter 12.]

"It has been my observation that ownership investing produces about twice the total return of lender investing. In some periods, this is clear from the simple raw numbers. In others, you need to extract inflation from the numbers to see the true results."

Grandpa handed another piece of paper to Jamie. "Look at this. During the seventy-six years from 1926 through 2001, the S&P 500 total average return was 10.7 percent. That was almost twice that of long-term U.S. government bonds' return of 5.8 percent. However, for the twenty years from 1982 through 2001, the S&P 500 return was 15.2 percent and the government bonds return was 12.1 percent, clearly not a 2-to-1 ratio."

two types of investments

Investment Returns: 76/20 Years Comparison
(Rate of return per annum compounded annually)

	76 Years 1926–2001	20 Years 1982–2001
Common Stocks	10.7%	15.2%
Government Bonds (long-term)	5.8%	12.1%
U.S. Treasury Bills	3.8%	6.1%
Average rate of inflation	3.1%	3.2%

Inflation-Adjusted Comparison

	76 Years Low Inflation	20 Years High Inflation
Common Stocks	7.0%	11.5%
Government Bonds (long-term)	1.8%	8.5%
U.S. Treasury Bills	0.4%	2.7%

"Now let's look at what happens when we adjust for the effects of inflation. Can you tell me what happens?"

Jamie studied the paper for a moment or two and then took a calculator off Grandpa's desk. After punching some buttons, Jamie said, "Adjusted for inflation, common stocks during the seventy-six-year period returned 3.89 times what government bonds returned." Jamie punched the calculator some more. "And adjusted for inflation, common stocks during the twenty-year period returned 1.35 times what government bonds returned. That's not even near double."

"Impressive," Grandpa said, thoroughly convinced that his grandchild was nothing less than a genius. "You can see why you must be careful when accepting generalizations such as 'ownership investing yields about twice the total return of lender investing.'"

Grandpa handed Jamie a chart showing a comparison of

the ratio of total returns over different time frames. "From a high of 3.89-to-1 down to a low of 1.35-to-1 is quite a range. Choosing other periods will yield other ratios, but I still contend that ownership investing will yield a much better total return than lender investing, even if the ratio varies."

"And about 2-to-1 is not a bad generalization," Jamie added, "if you understand what generalizations are." Grandpa smiled.

Inflation-Adjusted Total Returns of the S&P 500 Compared to Long-Term Government Bonds

Periods	S&P 500	Long-Term Government Bonds	Ratio
20 Years			
'73–'92	4.8%	2.7%	1.8 to 1
'74–'93	6.5%	4.0%	1.6 to 1
'75–'94	8.7%	3.8%	2.3 to 1
'76–'95	8.9%	4.9%	1.8 to 1
'77–'96	9.0%	4.2%	2.1 to 1
'78–'97	11.0%	5.1%	2.2 to 1
'79–'98	12.3%	6.0%	2.1 to 1
'80–'99	13.3%	6.3%	2.1 to 1
'81–'00	11.5%	8.0%	1.4 to 1
'82–'01	11.5%	8.5%	1.4 to 1
76 Years			
'26–'01	7.0%	1.8%	3.89 to 1

two types of investments

"Now let's discuss some terms to make sure you and I are talking about the same things," Grandpa said.

"The word *ownership* could also be used interchangeably with the word *equity*. For example, people refer to that portion of the dollar amount of ownership in their home as the equity they have in their home. This dollar amount of equity consists of both their down payment and the portion of their monthly mortgage payments that pay off the principal, plus or minus the appreciation or depreciation."

"Got it," Jamie said.

"Furthermore," Grandpa continued, "the words *lend* or *lender* should be associated with a fixed-dollar investment. You invest a fixed amount. You are returned this fixed amount plus interest. You might allow your interest to accumulate, but even in this case, you are returned your original investment plus interest."

Jamie looked a bit puzzled, so Grandpa explained further. "The original amount you invest as a lender never appreciates or depreciates in value. It remains fixed. As an aside, the current market value (the amount at which you could sell this fixed investment) will fluctuate as interest rates on new fixed investments (bonds and such) go up and down. For example, say you bought a ten-year bond that pays an interest rate of 5 percent. Two years later ten-year bonds are available that pay a 6 percent interest rate. Since no one would be interested in buying your 5 percent bond if they could receive 6 percent on a new one, the original bond could only be sold if it is offered for less than the original price. However, upon maturity (the ten-year period in this case) this bond would be redeemed for the original price. You get back exactly what you put in, plus interest.

"If you invest the same amount of money in shares of stock, the value of the stock can appreciate or depreciate, regardless of whether any interest or dividends have been paid. When you sell, you might get back more than you put in or you might get back less.

"I also should say a word about the fundamental ratio of

risk to reward. First, all investments have both risk and reward. Ownership-equity investments have both more risk and more potential reward than lender-fixed investments. The longer you can leave the money invested, the closer the risk for an equity investment comes to the risk for a fixed investment.[6] Also, with an equity investment, you have the potential for a much larger reward than you do with a fixed investment."

"What is the best risk-reward ratio to aim for?" Jamie asked.

"It's almost impossible to hit the bull's-eye of your goals when you are aiming at the wrong target," Grandpa replied. "In an attempt to avoid risk in your investment portfolio, you might place too much of your money in savings investments, such as CDs, Treasury bills, bonds, or bond mutual funds. When you do this, you may be aiming at the wrong target. All you really are doing is attempting to protect the "face amount" of your investment, the amount you initially put in—the principal. As Will Rogers use to say, 'You are more interested in a return *of* your money than a return *on* your money.'

"You use savings investments because you are interested primarily in protecting the principal of your investment. You probably will be successful, but if you are, then you are aiming at and hitting the wrong target.

"Of course, the worst risk you can take is one where you risk not getting any of your money back. Many people decide that if they can at least get their money back, they've been prudent. But these people do not take into account the possibility that they may have to live with considerably reduced purchasing power.

"If you don't believe inflation will go away, then you should want to avoid risk by aiming at the protection of your purchasing power, not just the protection of your principal."

Grandpa made a sketch on a piece of paper and showed it to Jamie. "You can go from a complete loss of your money near one end of this graph to an inflation-adjusted return of your money near the opposite end."

The Centering Mentality

←———————————|————————————→

Complete Loss   Return   Inflation-Adjusted
of Money   of Money   Return of Money

"There are many ways to experience a complete loss of your money. Gambling on a regular basis is one obvious way, as is loss through fraud or by theft. Any of these experiences is worse than a mere complete return of your money. Over time, however, the effective difference between a complete loss of your money and a mere return on your money becomes less and less."

Grandpa pulled another graph from his file drawer and gave it to Jamie.

Time-Adjusted Purchasing Power

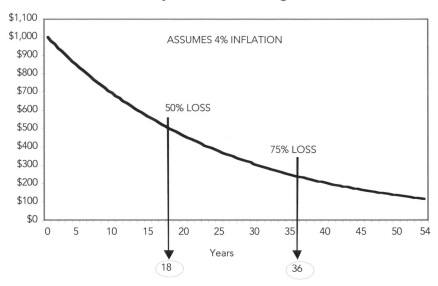

"As you can see," continued Grandpa, "over time the loss of your purchasing power approaches a complete loss of your money. They both have virtually the same effect on your standard of living. It is certainly not good to suffer a 50 percent loss in the purchasing power of your money in just eighteen years, or a 75 percent loss in thirty-six years."

Jamie studied the graph and had a new question. "How much would someone need to have to avoid this kind of erosion of his or her savings?"

Grandpa took one more graph from his file drawer.

Time-Adjusted Purchasing Power II

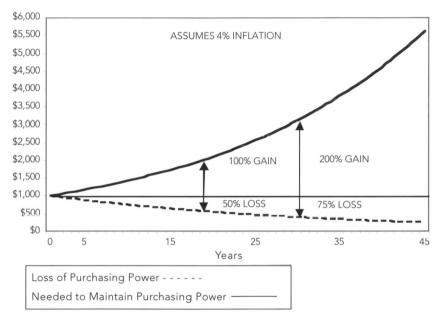

"Suppose inflation averages 4 percent a year," Grandpa began. "You will need to double your asset base in eighteen years or quadruple it in thirty-six years just to stay even. This is just to maintain your purchasing power with no improvement.

"Some people think of themselves as being averse to taking any risks. They should make sure they understand what their risks really are. Their ultimate risk might very well be the loss of purchasing power. Remember, as the data show, over time the loss of purchasing power approaches the total loss of one's investment dollars. So, if you want to defend yourself against this risk, you must be sure to aim at the right target when you invest assets."

"Let me see if I got it," Jamie said. "There are two kinds of investments—ownership, also called equity type, and lender, also called fixed type. A wise investor will have some of each, but much more equity than fixed."

"Right so far," Grandpa smiled.

"Now to determine how good an investment is," Jamie continued, "you must look at the total return. Total return is a combination of income—that's dividends or interest—plus appreciation of the amount invested."

Grandpa nodded.

"Then you talked about something called risk-reward ratio," Jamie went on. "I'm not so sure on this, but I think every investment has both. One of the biggest risks is the loss of purchasing power from inflation. This type of loss affects fixed investments more than equity investments."

Jamie paused and then asked, "How did I do?"

"Very well," Grandpa replied. "I think you just summarized your next research paper for school."

"Not quite, Grandpa," Jamie said. "I still need to know how much to invest in equity and how much in fixed."

"That is called asset allocation," replied Grandpa, "but first we need to discuss the different categories of investments. We can cover that another time. I think we have done enough for one day."

"Agreed," said Jamie. "Besides, I'm hungry. Have enough assets to treat me to lunch?"

"You betcha!" replied Grandpa.

notes

1. The Rule of 72 is a rule-of-thumb shortcut to determine how long it will take to double a sum of money at a given interest rate with annual

compounding. You divide 72 by the rate. For example: $72 \div 7 = 10$. Therefore, \$10,000 @ 7 percent would become \$20,000 in about 10 years. Actually, it would take closer to 10.285711429 years, and even this is an approximation, because $72 \div 7$ does not come out even. Other examples: $72 \div 8 = 9$; $72 \div 6 = 12$; $72 \div 5 = 14.4$.

2. Yield is the profit or return derived from an investment and usually is stated as a rate at which an investment pays out interest or dividends. Yield percentages are stated in annual terms. Certificates of Deposit (CDs) are often said to have an *annual interest rate*, which is the percentage of interest the CD pays, and a higher *effective annual yield*, which is the actual amount of interest if the principal and interest remain on deposit for the full term of the certificate.

3. $\$0.20 \div \$10.00 = 0.02$, or 2 percent.

4. $\$1.05 \div \$10.00 = 0.105$, or 10.5 percent.

5. An investment company that pools its shareholders' money to invest in a diversified group of stocks, bonds, money-market securities, and other types of investments according to the policies and objectives set forth in the fund's prospectus.

6. At least this has been true historically. Earlier in this chapter, you saw the data for investing in the stock market only during down years. If the investor has the time to wait—that is, to leave the money invested—the losses eventually are more than compensated for by substantial gains.

chapter 11

The Adventures of
Jamie and Grandpa, Part 2:
Six Places to Store Your Wealth

The senior citizen had just returned to his den with a freshly made cup of tea when his favorite grandchild burst through the front door.

"Grandpa, are you here?" shouted Jamie. "I'm ready for our next session. You know, the one about different investment categories." Jamie bounded into the den. "Oh, there you are."

"You have a good memory," Grandpa said, as he walked around his desk, carefully placed the full teacup on a coaster atop the desk, and then collapsed into his favorite leather chair.

"I have to have a good memory if I'm going to be rich like you someday," Jamie teased. "Let's get started!"

"Well," Grandpa began, "I like to put all investments into six different groups: cash, stock market, real estate, precious metals, collectibles, and tax-favored."

"You make it sound like I should take notes," Jamie said, flopping onto the couch opposite Grandpa's desk.

"Take notes?" Grandpa exclaimed. "What about your famous memory?"

"Stop kidding around and tell me about these categories and how much I should put into each of them."

"Okay, let's start with the places you might put your money," Grandpa replied. "Later we'll talk about how much to put in each of them."

Grandpa pushed a small poster across the desktop.

CASH

If you have too much,
inflation will destroy you.

If you have too little,
you will destroy
your other investments.

"The cash category," Grandpa said, "includes all available currency, including the coins and bills you have with you right now or that you've stuffed in your piggy bank at home. It also includes all the fixed-dollar investments we discussed last time. One obvious example is an interest-bearing savings account by which you lend your money to a bank. The purpose of cash is to provide stability, liquidity, availability, and low to very low risk of loss of your invested dollar."

"Let me check this out," Jamie interrupted. "Stability means I avoid big ups and downs in value. Liquidity means I have the ability to get my money back fast. Availability means that I can get the cash easily, such as walking into a local bank, making a telephone call, or writing a letter. Low risk means that I can expect to get out at least what I put in."

"I couldn't have said it better," Grandpa said. "Remember, the big risk in the cash category is the loss of purchasing power. The major reward is the availability of money for emergencies and other investment opportunities. When the investment that is right for you comes along, it would be a shame to miss the opportunity simply because you didn't have enough cash on hand."

"So I should always keep a substantial amount of cash," Jamie said.

"Not necessarily," Grandpa replied. "Generally, the more

available your money is in a cash investment, the lower the interest rate you will earn. Let's start with the cash in your pocket, piggy bank, or non-interest-bearing accounts. These are the most liquid, but they provide you with a zero return."

"Who would put money into a bank account that pays no interest?" Jamie asked. "That doesn't seem too smart."

"Actually, a lot of people have their money in such accounts," Grandpa said. "They are called checking accounts, and rather than pay interest, some checking accounts can even cost you money."[1]

Grandpa continued. "The next step up is savings accounts or money-market accounts. At this level, the quality of the institution becomes a factor. The concept is simple: The higher the quality of the savings institution, the lower the rate of return, or interest, you receive on your money."

Jamie jumped in. "And the greater your risk, the higher the rate of return."

"Exactly," Grandpa replied. "For example, Treasury bills, or T-bills, are short-term[2] savings vehicles backed by the full faith and credit of the United States government. Since Uncle Sam has the power to tax all of its citizens up to all of their income and assets, the credit rating or quality of the U.S. government is the best. Because of that, such investments typically have the lowest rates of return. At the opposite end of the spectrum would be banks or credit unions that are in danger of failing. It's a continuum."

Grandpa made a quick sketch and showed it to Jamie.

Highest Quality Institution   Lowest Quality Institution

←――――――――――――――――――――――→

Lowest Interest Rate   Highest Interest Rate

"The next important factor is how long you are willing to lend your money," Grandpa continued. "The longer you commit your money, the greater the return. The U.S. government borrows money on those T-bills I mentioned for up to 365 days. But you can lend your money to the government and receive a promissory note called a Treasury note. The time periods can be up to ten years. Other notes, called Certificates of Deposit—CDs—or time certificates, are issued by banks and usually pay a higher rate of return when you commit your cash for a longer period. The U.S. government also borrows money on a very long-term basis in the form of U.S. government bonds.

"Almost all major corporations also borrow money and issue pieces of paper that state their promises to pay certain rates of interest for specific periods of time. This long-term lending on your part increases the interest you earn—your reward—but it also means the money is not available to you. More important, it increases the potential loss of purchasing power—your risk—depending on the length of time and the amount of inflation.

"There is a so-called secondary market where long-term notes, bonds, CDs, and so forth can be sold prior to the maturity date. The actual dollar amount received, however, can be different than the amount invested. This introduces an investment phenomenon that I call the teeter-totter effect."

"Teeter-totters I understand," Jamie said.

"Let's use just one bond for our example. Here's the basic rule. As other interest rates on newer bonds decline, the price of the original bond goes up; as other interest rates go up, the price of the original bond goes down. During the 1980s, interest rates fell from the mid-teens to the 4 to 8 percent range, depending on time to maturity and the risk rating of the investment."

Grandpa sketched two seesaws on a piece of paper.

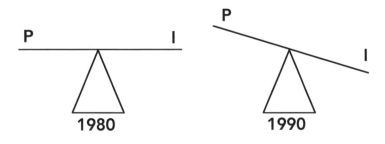

"Now, if the letter P stands for the price of the bond and the letter I stands for the interest," Grandpa explained, "you can see in this picture how the rule produces the teeter-totter effect. Had you purchased bonds in 1980, you would have received a double-digit yield during the next decade while watching the value of your bonds increase in the market."

Grandpa stopped as he noticed Jamie's raised hand.

"I don't understand that," Jamie said. "If interest rates were falling during the decade, how could I be earning a double-digit yield? And how would I receive, at the same time, an increase in value on the bonds?"

"Let's take a look at the interest situation first," Grandpa replied. "When you invest in a bond, you get a piece of paper with the title *Bond*. Also printed on this piece of paper is the interest rate that you will receive during the term of the investment. This interest rate does not change. If you hold the bond to maturity, you get back what you paid for it, and you have earned the promised interest all along.

"If your bond appreciates in value, the only way you can receive this appreciated value is to sell the bond. You may or may not choose to do this."[3]

Grandpa made another sketch on the piece of paper.

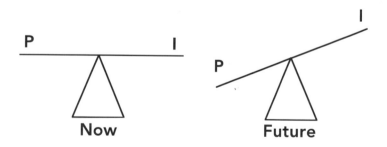

"Keep in mind, Jamie, that the teeter-totter can totter the other way. When interest rates go back up, the value of your bond goes down."

six places to store your wealth

"The important point to remember is that you can lose money on bonds if you have to sell them before their maturity date—when their value is lower than what you paid. Value can fall, for example, after interest rates in general have risen. You can make money, on the other hand, if you sell bonds when their value is greater than what you paid; value can increase after interest rates in general have fallen."

Grandpa continued. "The bond is a legal contract executed between two or more parties. It is called an indenture. Always read your bond indenture carefully. It may contain a key provision known as a *call provision*. A call provision is a right that the issuer of the bond has reserved to demand that you sell the bond back to the issuer after a stated date and at a stated price. This price could be the initial cost of the bond or a higher value. If the issuer calls the bond as of a certain date, interest stops on that date and you will receive payment for surrendering the bond.

"One final note," Grandpa added. "We're talking here about high-quality bonds, not junk bonds, which are low-quality, high-risk bonds with a greater likelihood that the issuer of the bond will default. Unless you want as many gray hairs as I have, we'll skip those in your retirement planning."

Grandpa took a sip of his tea and then summarized: "The cash category includes all fixed-dollar investments in which you are a lender. These investments include actual cash, savings accounts, CDs, T-bills, money-market accounts, government and corporate bonds, fixed-dollar annuities, and fixed-dollar life insurance.[4]

"Mortgages, personal loans, and other accounts receivable[5] are also cash-type holdings, but there usually are other considerations involved with each. For example, a mortgage is usually backed with improved real estate. If the borrower defaults on the loan, then the lender can become the owner of the property, which then removes the investment from the cash category and places it into the real-estate category. Another example is when parents or grandparents lend money to children; it often becomes a gift rather than a loan. Then it is no longer a financial asset at all."

"Okay," said Jamie. "I've got it. Now what are the other categories?"

Grandpa handed another small poster to Jamie.

STOCK

Ownership creates wealth.
The stock market represents
ownership.

"The second category is investments in the stocks of businesses that have decided to sell ownership interests in their corporation.

"Investing in the stock market has been a very effective method of developing wealth. This category, as represented by the Standard & Poor's 500 Index, has provided extensive return on investment. For example, during the seventy-six years between January 1, 1926, and December 31, 2001, the average annual return was 10.7 percent. As we discussed in our last session [see Chapter 10], there were twenty-two years of negative returns during this period, and fifty-four years of positive returns. During those seventy-six years we have seen depression, wars, the rise and fall of Communism, and a change in our standard of living greatly in excess of all the preceding years of recorded history of mankind.

"The stock market has been analyzed as much or more than any other investment category, and there probably are equal amounts of silly and sensible theories on why this or that happened. There are more so-called experts in the stock market than just about anywhere else. Yet one of the wisest of them all, Sir John Marks Templeton, says, 'I've never met anyone who could consistently predict the ups and downs of the stock market.'

"Templeton did very well with a mutual fund he started on November 30, 1954. If you had invested $10,000 in the Templeton Growth Fund at its inception, this amount, reduced by a sales charge, would have become worth $3,477,652 by December 31, 2001.[6] This is an average annual return of 14.3 percent and is 1.6 percent greater than the S&P 500 average for the same period.

"It is always possible to find another fund or group of stocks that did better than, not as well as, or almost the same as the S&P 500, and I could use one of these for comparing the performance of the stock market with other types of investments. But professional and individual investors have been using the S&P 500 as a measure of stock performance for more than seventy-six years. It is widely reported on television, radio, and in newspapers all across the country, so it is available daily to you, Jamie, and to virtually every other interested person. So, I will use the S&P 500 as a benchmark for any comparisons we discuss. The media often report on the Dow Jones Industrial Average, but professionals prefer the S&P 500 because it is a broader index."

"How would I invest in the stock market, Grandpa?" asked Jamie.

"There are two fundamental methods of investing," Grandpa replied. "One way is to purchase individual stocks. The other is to invest in pooled accounts. The most popular type of pooled account is the mutual fund, as we discussed the last time we met, which I'll refer to as buying mutual funds.[7]

"I don't recommend that you, or any individual, purchase individual stocks. There is a story, no doubt apocryphal, that makes an important point. It goes this way. It used to take three days for information about actions in Washington, D.C., to reach the New York Stock Exchange. Today it takes three seconds. Immediately after getting this information, the big guys—those responsible for the pension plans, the college endowment funds, the bank and insurance companies' stock market investment portfolios, and the mutual funds—make their moves to lock in the profits or avoid the losses implied by the information.

"You and I, Jamie, and a lot of other people, will read or hear the news from Washington minutes, hours, or even days later—long after the market has already made its adjustment to the news. Even the Internet's almost instant access to information requires an individual to be on line at the exact time the news breaks. Amateurs in any field seldom can compete with professionals. When it comes to investments, leave it to the pros. Don't compete with them. Join them."

"Okay," Jamie agreed. "But what fund should I invest in?"

"That's the beauty of mutual funds," Grandpa answered. "A mutual fund attempts to minimize the risk by investing in various companies according to the fund's objectives. The beauty is that you can invest in several different funds with different goals. This really helps to minimize the risk in a way that you could never afford otherwise."

"How many funds should I consider?" Jamie asked.

"Six to eight, I'd say," Grandpa answered. "That would give you ample diversification in both stocks and investment counsel.[8] Any more than six to eight and you would bump into yourself. You would have one of your funds buying stock XYZ while another would be selling it. Your investment position in stock XYZ stays the same; all you've done is run up transaction costs. Even with eight funds, you may have some of this, but the need for diversification in investment advice is overriding.

"Be careful now, Jamie," cautioned Grandpa. "Mutual funds come in both equity type (stock market) and fixed-dollar type (cash, bonds, and such). Make sure that you allocate the type of fund you have to the correct category—cash or stock market.

"You can divide the stock market into four subcategories: growth and income; growth; small-capitalization companies; and international. There could be a fifth subsection called aggressive growth, but extra study is needed if you wish to include this type."

"What's the difference between income stocks and growth stocks?" Jamie asked. "Which one would make me more money?"

"You can make money both ways," Grandpa said, "but in the jargon of investing, income and growth refer to two different approaches to making money. Income stocks refer to stocks of companies that are expected to make impressive profits and pay extensive dividends. Growth stocks refer to stocks that are expected to increase in value over time but not necessarily pay large or even any dividends. Profits are received when you sell the stocks."

"I see," said Jamie. "That means that growth-and-income stocks are those that are expected to pay dividends as well as increase in value. Now, what are small-capitalization companies?" asked Jamie.

"As the name implies," replied Grandpa, "these are companies that are small in that they have a smaller amount of capital backing them."

"You mean they might not have enough money to make a go of it?" asked Jamie.

"No," Grandpa smiled, "they probably have enough money, or at least they believe they do. It's simply that the amount they have backing them is small when compared to the amounts backing giants like General Motors or Microsoft. Somewhere among these smaller companies is where you will find the next giants if they are as successful as they hope to be."

"And I guess international is sort of obvious" Jamie said. "These are companies in countries other than the United States, right?"

"Right," replied Grandpa. "Global investing is a must. Back in 1970, two-thirds of all stocks were issued by companies based in the United States. Today, two-thirds are companies based outside the United States. If you are in a position to be reasonably aggressive in this category, you should invest some of your money in mutual funds of small-capitalization companies in small countries around the world. Such stocks just might out-perform all others.

"The cost of operating these funds is greater, but the net results could also be better. While traveling in Singapore in 1993, my guide made the statement, 'If you pay peanuts, you get monkeys.' This can apply to almost everything, including mutual funds. When your financial future is involved, you should not be looking for bargains in management fees. Certain expertise costs more. Of course, you don't want to overpay for anything.

"Here's another 'should not.' I believe that you should not invest in sector funds."

"What are those?" Jamie asked.

"A sector fund is one that invests exclusively in one something-or-other. One country. One industry. One commodity. That type of thing. At certain times, one country might have a superior appreciation. This happened with Japan in the 1980s. But the problem is to know when to get out. It's just as difficult as owning individual stocks and knowing when to sell. The proper time to sell requires extensive research, considerable expertise, and a whole lot of foresight, which might be called luck.

"Even the professionals—who spend full-time and have masses of information at their fingertips—have a difficult time. If the pros have a hard time, then the amateur must rely on an extraordinary amount of good fortune. If you must gamble, I suggest that you take a very small amount of your wealth and visit Las Vegas, Lake Tahoe, or Atlantic City. All are happy to accept your money."

Grandpa pulled out another small poster and gave it to Jamie.

REAL ESTATE
Buy land.
They ain't making any more.

"Now we come to real estate. This category includes your personal residence, perhaps a secondary residence, and vacant land that you might own. I include rental real estate in the tax-favored category, so we'll discuss it later.

"Many, if not most, textbooks do not include personal real estate as an investment category. They justify this omission by saying that your home is not producing income and that you have to live somewhere. This omission is an appalling error. For the vast majority of people, their personal real estate represents the most important asset they have. Real estate can appreciate quite a bit, and often the excess value when it is sold represents a significant profit that can be reallocated in other investment categories.

"For example, some people want to move to a smaller home when they retire. The profit they get from selling the old home can be used to buy a new home, and the leftover money can be put into other appropriate investments.

"There is another important aspect of including personal real estate in this category of investments. We want to make sure it is considered when we look at whether you have allocated enough or too much of your wealth to personal-use real estate. [See Chapter 12.] A lot of people do not think of their own home as a real estate investment. It is—a very important one.

"Starting in the second half of the 1980s, real estate of all kinds—and in most but not all places—was in a long-term decline of its investment cycle. In the 1990s, the cycle started to reverse itself. The dumping of a considerable amount of real estate during the savings and loan bailout[9] plus a tightening of credit caused the expected cyclical recovery to be very slow in coming.

"The combination of eight to ten years of declining values, the bailout, over-construction during the preceding decade, and tight credit discouraged new construction. Also, high vacancy rates depressed rental rates. Many owners were struggling to make profits. However, this situation was cyclical, and it eventually changed, as the housing supply can't keep up with the demand for housing. In the future, I believe, owners of real estate will see a significant increase in the value of their properties and realize nice profits when they sell."

"How do you know when to buy real estate, Grandpa?" Jamie asked.

"That's a lot like asking me when to buy stock," Grandpa replied. "No one can consistently predict the bottoms or tops of cycles. Still, I feel strongly that any adults currently renting their residence should make every effort to buy. Rents on a relative basis will go sky-high in the future.

"The risk in buying is that property taxes will rise substantially in the future, but the reward is affordable housing and an increase in value. Remember, as far as taxes are concerned, a renter pays the property tax as part of the rent, so all future tax increases will be paid by an increase in rent."

"I think I've got it," said Jamie, "except for that bailout thing. But I can look that up. What's the next category?"

"The next two categories are currently of minor importance," Grandpa answered. "One is precious metals, and the other is collectibles."

Out came two more small posters.

PRECIOUS METALS

Like life insurance,
when you don't need it,
it's easy to get;

when you do need it,
it's not available at any price.

"Precious metals include gold, silver, platinum, and the like. You can purchase these metals in the form of coins or bars. The first rule is: Pay cash and take possession. Scams can take place when you allow someone you do not know to store the metals.

Sometimes this is an empty promise, and all you have for your investment is a very impressive-looking certificate.

"Various governments, including the U.S. government, mint silver coins and gold coins in various weights up to one ounce. These coins are available from reputable dealers across the country. Some dealers also make available bars of metal in weights above one ounce. All are priced close to the current bullion rate, that is, the current market rate of these metals.

"Another rule about precious metals: Don't buy stocks in gold or silver mines. That is simply a stock market investment. You don't own the metal itself. You also have made a sector investment, which, as I noted earlier, is not recommended.

"So far, the only universal currency we have is precious metals. Over the next couple of decades, this may change, but for now, this bullion has international respect and could substantially increase in importance and value in a serious global financial crisis."

COLLECTIBLES
Enjoy them
or
forget them.

"Collectibles include rare coins and stamps, top-quality diamonds, oriental rugs, fine paintings, artifacts, and antiques. These are items that are expected to increase in value over very long periods of time. My feeling is that these investments are for your heirs or their heirs, since it might take forty years or more for them to acquire any substantial appreciation. You should only purchase those items that you will enjoy viewing or those that represent a hobby, such as a rare-stamp collection.

"Be careful. Only top-quality items will significantly increase in value, and proper selection requires a very high level of knowledge about each item. Always obtain quality advice from a specialist in a specific collectible. This advice is worth the cost of consultation.

"It's not unusual for a painting to have a price tag of ten thousand dollars, but have a real value of much less than that. The value of a diamond is determined by its size and shape, but more important, by its quality. To evaluate the quality of a diamond requires knowledge and experience acquired only after many years of study and experience. The quality of a rare coin, rare stamp, or rare anything is an important attribute of its value and, in most cases, can be determined only by an expert.

"Sure, some people have ignored this advice and still made a nice profit. I have a friend who purchased a rare gold coin for a quarter of a million dollars and sold it for a million. I have another friend who bought a rare automobile for fifty thousand dollars and sold it for two hundred thousand. Both sales were within a decade of the purchase. Both friends took these actions on a whim without professional advice. And both were extremely lucky and learned the wrong lesson: how easy it is to make profits in collectibles." Grandpa smiled, and then continued.

"Of course, I'm sure I also have other friends who made similar purchases and lost bundles of money. They're just not that eager to tell me their stories."

"I wonder why?" Jamie said. "Well, Grandpa, we still have one more category to cover."

"Correct," Grandpa said, handing Jamie another small poster.

TAX-FAVORED

Some of your investments
should have a tax advantage,
at least until taxation disappears.

"The last category is tax-favored investments. This category actually includes investments in the first three categories: cash, stock market, and real estate. But to qualify for the tax-favored classification, each must have at least one tax advantage. There are three kinds of tax advantages: deductible, deferred, and exempt."

Jamie frowned, so Grandpa explained.

"Tax deductible means you do not pay income tax on that portion of your income. Examples include contributions to retirement plans such as an IRA, 401(k), 403(b), pensions, profit sharing, and 457 plans. Rental real estate also provides for deductions from your income for depreciation of the property. Natural resources, such as oil and gas, allow a depletion deduction. There are restrictions and requirements involved in these examples, but there is no need to go into them right now.

"Tax deferral means that, in general, you can postpone paying taxes on income or profits. You pay no tax, for example, on the profits you earn in retirement plans until you retire and begin to withdraw the funds.[10] As your real estate appreciates in value, you pay no tax on the appreciation until you sell the property. This applies to your personal home and to any rental properties you own.[11]

"Other examples include annuities, life insurance, EE Bonds,[12] and unrealized capital appreciation of stocks or mutual funds."

At that moment both of Jamie's hands shot up.

"Don't worry about understanding all of this. Just be aware of the fact that tax-deferred investments do exist. The details can be examined when you are ready to consider one or more such investments. Besides, by then the rules may change.

"We still have one more advantage to mention. Tax exempt means that you do not have to pay any tax on the income from the investment. Municipal bonds are a good example. Interest from U. S. government T-bills, T-notes, and T-bonds is exempt from state and local taxation but not from federal taxation. The Roth IRA is another example of tax-exempt investments. You must meet certain qualifications, but if you do, you receive all the accumulated profits tax-free.

"The amount of income taxation changes from time to time, but the top tax bracket has been 50 percent or greater in sixty-three out of the eighty-nine years from 1913 through 2001, and it has been 70 percent or greater in fifty out of these same eighty-nine years."

Grandpa handed a small poster with a graph on it to Jamie.

Maximum Income Tax Rates

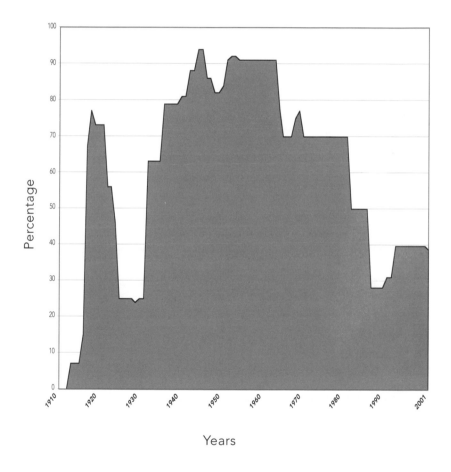

Years

"Since the amount of taxation is subject to the will—some say whim—of our various elected government representatives,

six places to store your wealth

some degree of agility on your part is important. Your readiness and ability to change your asset allocation will enhance your profits considerably. Most top-performing investments take time to appreciate, and your willingness to stay with these wisely selected vehicles is important. Should the taxation climate change, so should you change.

"Starting in 1987, I recommended to certain friends that they stop or greatly reduce contributions to their retirement plans. This allowed them to obtain a better-balanced portfolio. At a maximum 28 percent tax bracket, their tax deduction and tax deferral advantage became less important than their improperly balanced portfolio. But when the top bracket went to 31 percent in 1991, we had to reconsider this action, but for most, this 3 percent increase remained secondary to a properly balanced portfolio. In 1993, when the top bracket rose to 39.6 percent, very serious re-evaluation had to take place.

"It's always difficult to stop putting assets in investments with tax savings. However, in 1987, I saw a window of opportunity to improve diversification. I believed that 28 percent was not likely to last very long as the top bracket. My friends' accountants were in total disagreement with my recommendation because their view was narrow and focused only on the tax situation. When I presented them with the concept of the importance of having a properly balanced investment portfolio, most of the accountants acquiesced.

"Now, after the fact, the friends who took my advice recognize certain advantages in giving up a deduction when in a low tax bracket. Unfortunately, those friends who did not take my advice now wish a similar opportunity would reappear. Personally, I believe the opportunity may have been a once-in-a-lifetime occurrence for many retirees, although I hope I'm wrong. The point is that you must stay as alert and flexible as possible.

"And now, Jamie, I don't know about you, but I'm ready for a nap." Grandpa got to his feet, stretched slowly so as not to surprise any of his muscles, and then started toward the kitchen.

"No review?" asked Jamie. "No summary?"

"Later," Grandpa said. "There will be plenty of time later for more. Take too much into your brain without a break and it'll start spilling out your ears. Now, come along."

notes

1. Service charges on checking accounts can be a monthly fee or fixed fees per check or even per deposit. Checking accounts provide you with an easy way to transfer funds quickly from one place to another. They also provide you with a concrete record of such transfers. There are checking accounts that do pay a small amount of interest if you maintain a minimum balance. There also are mutual funds that have checking privileges, although some restrictions may apply. Which type of account or combination of accounts is right for you is your choice, but it should be made only after careful study and consideration.

2. Up to 365 days.

3. The call date, or the date when the bond matures, can affect the value of the bond. Generally a call date any time in the near future decreases the market value of the bond.

4. Fixed-dollar annuities and fixed-dollar life insurance also could be in the category of tax-favored, which will be discussed later in this chapter.

5. Accounts receivable are often connected to the sale of something and, therefore, can be affected by the many considerations of a trade or business.

6. This growth includes all dividends and distributed capital gains reinvested.

7. Other pooled accounts are closed-end funds and wrap accounts, which I do not recommend for various reasons. Also, any two or more people can get together, pool their money and knowledge, and buy stocks. This, in a very real sense, is the same as a pooled account. Such groups or stock clubs, however, are not always available to everybody; mutual funds are.

8. Each mutual fund has one or more advisors or managers of the fund attempting to meet the goals of that fund. When you add more funds to your portfolio, you also add more advisors and managers. You not only have a diversification of stocks, you also have a diversification of professional advice.

9. During this period, a significant number of savings and loan associations

or banks became insolvent and had to be liquidated or taken over by other institutions. The Federal Savings and Loan Insurance Corporation (FSLIC) covered most deposits. The bailout ran into billions of taxpayers' dollars.

10. Some retirement plans allow early withdrawals prior to retirement for defined emergencies. Tax on the withdrawal is due at that time.

11. Even though it might seem proper to include a personal residence in the tax-favored category because of this one tax advantage, I believe it is much more important to assign it to a stand-alone, personal-use real estate category.

12. You have the option to pay annually or to defer the tax.

chapter 12

The Adventures of Jamie and Grandpa, Part 3: Investing Wisely

Grandpa carefully carried his freshly brewed cup of tea into his den and almost spilled it when a voice from behind startled him.

"Hi, Grandpa. I'm back."

Grandpa sat down behind his desk as Jamie continued without a pause. "I remember the two kinds of investments: ownership-equity and lender-fixed, and that ownership is far more important. I also remember the six different storage categories: cash, stock market, real estate, precious metals, collectibles, and tax-favored. Now, I'm ready to learn the how-much part."

"Your memory never ceases to amaze me," Grandpa said. "So, you must also know the three most important words in real estate."

"Sure," replied Jamie. "Location, location, and location."

"Correct," Grandpa said. "Now, do you know the three most important words for a proper investment portfolio?"

"Hmmm, I don't think so."

"Diversification, diversification, and diversification," Grandpa said. "I agree with Sir John Templeton[1] when he says that no one can consistently pick only winners. As we discussed before, I believe you should invest in the six different categories you just mentioned. But you should also diversify within each of these categories. There is no perfect ratio for the allocation of your assets, but the development of a model portfolio allocation can help you to meet your personal goals.

"Over the years, I have recommended the same initial asset allocation for nearly all of my friends. Naturally, the ranges of assets in each category can be adjusted to meet individual goals and temperament. However, those friends who stayed pretty close to the amounts I recommended obtained the least risky and most profitable investment portfolios.

"It might take some people years to rearrange their investments to get within these guidelines, but they should not be overly concerned about this. They shouldn't sell their present assets indiscriminately, causing unnecessary taxation or losses when a reasonable delay could avoid these negatives. But even major adjustments should be made at the earliest practical time if such changes are necessary to obtain a properly balanced portfolio. Of course, Jamie, you don't have this problem since you are just beginning to develop your portfolio."

Grandpa reached into his file drawer and pulled out a piece of paper. "Here, review this chart of asset allocation targets."

Jamie took the paper and studied the data.

Asset Allocation Targets

Category	Model Range	Pre-Retirement	Shortly After Retirement	Halfway Between Retirement and Age 100
Cash	10–20%	10%	15%	28%
Stock Market	15–25%	25+%	25+%	25+%
Real Estate	20–25%	25+%	25+%	20%
Precious Metals	1–4%	1-%	1-%	1-%
Tax Favored	20–38%	38-%	33-%	25%
Collectibles	0–5%	1-%	1-%	1-%

Key: + means "or more" and - means "or less"

"Let's discuss tax-favored investments first," Grandpa said. "You do remember the details on this category from our last session, don't you?" [See Chapter 11.] Jamie nodded and Grandpa continued. "I chose this category first because, as we discuss it, we also will note some principles that apply to all the categories in your portfolio.

"The tax-favored category should be low in cash and high in both the stock market and real estate. This means only a small portfolio of municipal bonds. I'm aware of the attraction of tax-free interest that municipal bonds hold for many people, but I'm equally aware of the loss of purchasing power. The risk or likelihood of losing purchasing power is far greater than the reward of tax savings. A small percentage invested in muni-bonds is proper in large estates, but until you have amassed your fortune, Jamie, muni-bonds should hold little interest for you.

"Fixed annuities—those that, unlike variable annuities, do not have a growth potential and only receive interest on the accumulated account value—also should be kept on the low side. The only exception to that would be in periods with extremely high interest rates. In the past, we have been able to lock in high, sometimes double-digit interest rates for as many as five and sometimes seven years. In such cases, we have the best of both worlds: a high rate of return without suffering a declining principal. In other words, we avoid the negative side of the teeter-totter effect discussed in our last session.

"Most retirement plans—such as an IRA, 401(k), 403(b), and some profit-sharing plans in the tax-favored category—allow the individual to select the investment vehicles. Asset allocation in retirement plans has been fairly consistent for many years for those people who have control over their retirement-plan investments. Studies show that these individuals in the past elected to have over 50 percent of their account or accounts in cash-type fixed-dollar investments.

"Now you should know, Jamie, that this percentage makes no financial sense at all. Retirement-plan investing is very long term—even a 50-year-old must consider that he or she can live for another fifty years—and over long periods of time, fixed-dollar investments have always performed in the vicinity of one-half that of equity investments.

"I'm sure, Jamie, you have read the ads or heard silly people say that you shouldn't take risks with your *serious* retirement money; you should place these accumulations in a savings account or some other fixed-dollar investment. But by doing this, you are taking the ultimate risk—the loss of your purchasing power with these serious dollars. You may think that you are earning three or four percent on these safe dollars when you might actually be losing two percent or more each and every year because of inflation.

"People should always invest their funds in something that will appreciate at a rate greater than the average rate of inflation. Invest in stock mutual funds or pooled real estate where you have both professional management and diversification."

"Is that what you did, Grandpa?" asked Jamie.

"Yes indeed," Grandpa replied.

"Are you still concentrating on assets that will appreciate?"

"Absolutely!"

"Even though you have partially retired?"

"Absolutely! In the early 1990s, the headlines of news-papers and TV news quoted retirees who complained that their standard of living had to be greatly reduced. It seems their CDs, which had been paying 10 percent or more, were now maturing, and the new CDs would only be paying 3 or 4 percent. They blamed this big drop in interest rates for their plight. Actually, they were the culprits because they elected to have all or a large por-tion of assets in fixed dollars.

"Some of these retirees had experienced an unusual double benefit from their bond investments. They had purchased qual-ity, high-yield, long-term corporate bonds in the early 1980s, and they had almost a decade of high interest payments *plus* an appreciating asset. The value or price of their bonds went up as general interest rates fell. At that point, they should have sold their bonds, taken their profits, and given thanks for having lived during such an unusual period.

"Instead, they were crying because the game was over. The time to sell old bonds is when the current interest yield on new bonds hits bottom. Sure, it's hard to sell a bond paying 10 percent or more, but that's how you play the fixed-dollar game. These retirees didn't know this, but now you do, Jamie. This phenomenon will probably never happen again in my lifetime, but it probably will in yours, and now you know how to play the game to win.

"Some investment advisors, especially those with an accounting background, recommend that you maximize the use of tax-favored investments. This can be a mistake. Keep in mind, Jamie, that the mere existence of this whole category of tax-favored investments is beyond your control. Our elected representatives have passed laws establishing tax favors, and they certainly have the power to change these laws any time it is to *their* advantage to do so. A good investment on Friday can be a bad investment on Monday because Washington changed its mind over the weekend."

"So, what is a maximum percentage of my portfolio that I might have in this category?" Jamie asked.

"That depends upon many things, Jamie," Grandpa answered. "But in general, I would say that if you put over one-third of your total investments in this category, you should consider carefully that something totally out of your control can suddenly change things to your disadvantage.

"When professional people first talk with me, I can guess their tax-favored allocation before actually seeing the numbers. If they are 50 years old or older, they consistently have 50 percent or more of their investments in the tax-favored category. I'm not surprised anymore to see 70 to 80 percent in this category. When the allocation becomes this great, it's usually impossible to properly reallocate, even given the remainder of their lifetimes.

"Remember, Jamie, our elected officials in Washington can do just about anything. In the summer of 1993, for example, they made tax increases retroactive to January 1 of that same year. For the first half of 1993, you were playing by their rules, which they later decided weren't their rules after all. Then they passed a law stating that a 15 percent income surtax would be applied to all withdrawals from retirement plans over a certain amount, cumulative for all your plans. And if you did not withdraw all your retirement investments during your lifetime, the extra 15 percent would be added to your tax rate for death taxes on this excess amount.

"This was major retroactive legislation. Because of this law, people have retired earlier than they wanted to, depriving our country of their talents and productivity. Some groups simply shut down their retirement plans, which created an even greater burden for their employees.

"In 1996, our legislators passed a new law that put a moratorium on the 15 percent tax for the years 1997, 1998, and 1999, and then they eliminated this silly surtax altogether. But who knows what they will do next?"

"So," Jamie interrupted, "if the rules can be changed anytime, even retroactively, then what am I supposed to do?"

"Just what you are doing. Learn as much as you can about everything that interests you. Be interested in everything. Keep in mind that rules about anything can be changed. For example, your school might increase the requirements for graduation, and you'd have to go to school for another whole year. Not likely, I admit, but possible. My point is that, because governments are always looking for ways to get more money, the tax-favored category of investments is more likely to experience rule changes than other areas.

"You must remember one thing. Greed is an investor's worst enemy, and the desire to reduce taxation often seduces one to overallocate investments in the tax-favored category. You also should remember that many tax favors granted by the government are simply just postponements of the taxes. When it comes time, and that time always comes eventually, you or your heirs will pay the piper, Uncle Sam.

"Now, let's get on with our allocations. When you develop your asset-allocation model, you should use percents. This model is called a 'common size' financial statement, and it makes it obvious when you have too much or too little in any category.

"Let's consider the category of real estate. Real estate is a good investment. It has been in the past and will be in the future. Real estate has its ups and downs, of course. What doesn't? And when you are in the declining cycle of any investment category, you are exposed to a great deal of pessimism, both in the media and from your well-meaning friends and colleagues. But when you have pessimism, you also have bargains. As Bernard Baruch said, 'Buy your straw hats in the winter time.' This is still good advice."

"Grandpa," Jamie interrupted, "what's this about straw hats?"

"I guess I'm showing my age," replied Grandpa, "and yours. Back when men always wore hats, they wore felt hats in winter and straw hats in the summer. Straw hats were cooler. Thus, a good time to buy . . . "

"I got it! I got it!" Jamie interrupted again. "Like in my economics class, we learned that when something is in great demand, the seller can get a better price. But when something is not wanted at all, or just by a few people, the seller has to lower the price to meet the minimum demand."

Grandpa smiled. Such a good grandchild—smart and fast and *his*.

"Let's continue, Grandpa," Jamie suggested.

"Ah, yes. Well, having said all those nice things about real estate and about buying during a down cycle, which is not bad advice about buying in any of the categories, by the way, I really

141   investing wisely

must caution you not to have too much of your wealth tied up in the real estate category. (See Appendix 3 for a Retirees Residence Feasibility Study.) If too much of your wealth is tied up in real estate for personal use—which for most people is their home—you will be missing growth in other areas.

"Let me explain. Over time, most real estate will appreciate. Owning your residence represents a growing asset. Your residence doesn't increase or decrease in value based just on the amount of your money invested in it. The appreciation is based on the total value, not just your equity. If when you buy a home you pay 20 percent of the total price as a down payment and borrow the balance, you are using an important investment concept called leverage.[2] This means that if your home appreciates in value, you benefit in multiples of your own investment.

"This might help you understand." Grandpa began writing some figures on a piece of paper while Jamie watched over his shoulder.

Purchase price	$100,000	$100,000	$100,000
Down payment	$100,000	$50,000	$20,000
Appreciated value	$200,000	$200,000	$200,000
Profit	$100,000	$150,000	$180,000
Appreciation on your investment	1 time or 100%	3 times or 300%	9 times or 900%

"Keep in mind that your profit is reduced by the cost of the borrowed money and the periodic repayments of principal. The multiples as an annual percentage are reduced by the elapsed time between purchase and sale, but the concept stays the same. This concept of using other people's money—OPM—can produce greater profits for you. Of course, it also can produce greater losses if the value of the property declines.

"The only time I recommend borrowing money is for your personal-use residence. Our tax laws, so far, continue to subsidize the expense of a mortgage on your personal residence by allowing you to deduct the interest you pay. This means that our government is paying a large portion of this expense by allowing this deduction.

"Let's get back to the proper percentage allocation for real estate. When you have more than 25 percent of your total investments tied up in personal-use real estate, it's possible that you either own too much real estate or you have not financed a large enough portion.

"Yes, I know the romantic story of burning the mortgage prior to retirement, and it is a good story. But if you live in a $250,000 house with no mortgage, you have $250,000 invested in personal-use real estate. Even if you have a $50,000 mortgage, then you still have $200,000 invested in this category. This investment may be appreciating in value, but it is providing you with no income until you sell. In these cases, if $250,000 or $200,000 is more than 25 percent of your wealth, then your income-producing assets may not be appreciating sufficiently to enable you to maintain your desired standard of living for a long life expectancy.

"What should you do? Well, if you can handle mortgage payments in the first case, you should consider obtaining a mortgage, and if you can handle greater payments in the second case, you should consider a larger mortgage, even if you are retired.

"The other side of this coin is where you have too small an amount of your wealth tied up in personal-use real estate. In this case, you should consider paying off all or part of your mortgage, if you have one, and then either purchasing a more expensive residence—if you can pay cash and if this would be desirable for you—or making improvements in your present residence that increase its value."

investing wisely

"This balancing act with regard to your personal-use real estate involves both a balanced investment portfolio as well as a balanced Cash Management Statement. [See Chapter 4.] Maybe of equal importance in all of this are your needs and desires for a residence. I recommend that you buy what you want, no more and no less, as long as you can afford it both now and for the remainder of your life.

"Now we come to the stock market. The range of 15 to 25 percent recommended for this category might be a bit misleading for two reasons. First, the 15 percent is recommended only for very low-risk-tolerant people, and only until they learn more about investing in diversified portfolios of stock mutual funds. Fifteen percent will not do the job we want done. It simply gives us a starting place. Second, even the upper limit of 25 percent is less than you should have because a healthy amount of the tax-favored category also should be in the stock market.

"There actually may be a third reason why the recommendation of 15 to 25 percent may be misleading. Because of the low percentage recommended for cash—10 percent prior to retirement and 15 percent early into retirement—and the 'or more' included in the stock market recommendation and the 'or less' included in the precious metals and collectibles recommendations, it is possible that you could have up to 50 percent of your total investments in the stock market well into retirement.

"On a daily basis, fluctuations in the stock market make this category the most obvious of all investments. Ups and downs in the market can be quite attention-grabbing, particularly as dramatically presented by the media. Such fluctuations can be unsettling to some people. But if you look at the history of the market, the longer the periods of time studied, the smaller the range of annual average total return becomes. In other words, over time, the ups and downs are not really so far up or so far down. You might also note that during any length of time studied, the average rate of return is fairly stable. Jamie, look at this chart."

The Stock Market 1933–1992

Length of Periods	Number of Periods	Minimum/ Maximum Total Returns	Spread	Average of All Periods
10 years	61	-0.1%/19.4%	19.5%	11.4%
20 years	51	4.4%/17.9%	13.5%	11.6%
25 years	46	7.9%/17.2%	9.3%	11.4%

"What the data show is that, historically at least, if you do not have to sell during a down period, the market has always come back up over time. You are young now, Jamie, and you have a lot of time to wait out any downs. When you get to be 70 years old, remember that you still might live another twenty-five, thirty, or more years. The odds are increasing all the time that this will be true. So you still have time to outwait down markets.

"In the cash category, I recommend 10 percent prior to retirement and then 15 percent into early retirement. I have been criticized by some investment advisors for this recommendation. They say these percentages are too small, especially for portfolio assets that should be income-producing.

"My defense against this charge is twofold. First, fixed-dollar investments cannot protect you from your worst financial enemy, inflation. Your rewards for being a lender are too small to produce both an income and an inflationary adjustment. Second, when you retire, you don't need an investment vehicle that produces income, such as is offered by fixed-dollar investments. All you need is cash flow, and it doesn't matter whether the cash flow is called dividends, interest, or principal."

"Grandpa," Jamie interrupted. "Are you saying that it's all right to spend principal in retirement?"

"Yes, I am, Jamie."

"But I've heard you say that many retired people come to you and say that spending principal is a sin, or at least a major no-no."

"Yes, they say that, but then I try to get them to look at it this way. Remember when we spoke about total return as meaning an investment income *plus* its appreciation?"

Jamie nodded assent.

"And we also talked about how total return is a better measurement to use than just investment income when comparing various opportunities for investments. Well, I tell my retired friends that it's the same concept when considering retirement income. If you let one investment appreciate and spend part of the principal from another investment, that part being no more than the first investment's appreciation, then what has happened to your total net worth?"

"That went by a little too fast for me, Grandpa."

"Okay, let's make up an example using easy numbers that make it simple." Grandpa started writing on another piece of paper. "Suppose you have two investments with $100,000 in each investment:

	Investment A	Investment B
Original principal	$100,000	$100,000

"And let's suppose that Investment A is paying dividends and also is appreciating in value so that at the end of one year, its total value is $112,000. Investment B, meanwhile, is earning interest at the rate of 5 percent.

	Investment A	Investment B
Original principal	$100,000	$100,000
Dividends or interest	$6,000	$5,000
Appreciation	$6,000	0
Value after 1 year	$112,000	$105,000

"Now, let's also suppose that at the end of the year you need an additional $6,000 to maintain your standard of living. From which investment would you take it?"

"Well," Jamie began, "I could take it from either investment. But if I take it from Investment A, then I could withdraw the dividends. If I take it from B, then I would have to use some principal."

"Wait a minute, Jamie," Grandpa interrupted this time. "You've made my point without even recognizing it." Jamie frowned. Grandpa continued. "Before you do anything more, how much are the two investments worth in all at the end of one year?"

"Together, they're worth $217,000."

"And how much will they be worth in all after you take out $6,000?"

"Together they will be worth $211,000."

"Regardless of where you take out the $6,000?"

"Oh, I get it now," Jamie exclaimed. "Whether I withdraw dividends or use some principal, the investments are still worth $211,000. What I decide to do is another question entirely."

"I wish some of my friends were as sharp as you." Grandpa beamed and then got serious again. "But we have to turn now to precious metals and collectibles, or you're never going to get home in time for supper."

"In time for *dinner*, Grandpa."

"Whatever," Grandpa snorted. "Anyway, most of my friends have about 1.5 percent of their total investments in precious metals, and about half of these friends have zero collectibles. The other half average about 3 percent in collectibles.

"I also have a friend who escaped from old Russia. She once asked me, 'What do you tell people about gold?' I answered that, in a time of crisis, gold could increase in purchasing power as much as ten times overnight. She waved her hand in front of my face and said, 'Wrong! One hundred times!'

"My Russian friend had a real-life experience to support her contention. If I thought that we, who live in a global society, were going to have a global financial crisis in the foreseeable future, I probably would be recommending 40 to 50 percent in precious metals instead of the 1 to 4 percent that I recommend. But I don't foresee such a calamity.

"Of all my friends, those who have significant investments in collectibles have expertise in a collectible, have a hobby in one area of collectibles, or enjoy rare artistic beauty. Maybe that's the way it should be.

"In spite of all the numbers we have been looking at, Jamie, an investment portfolio mix is more an art than a science. Sure, different financial experts have developed different ratios and formulas using all kinds of fancy calculations and have produced mixtures of risk-reward returns using alpha, beta, other coefficients, and the like. The bottom line for the vast majority of real people, such as you and me, is their comfort level with some of the tradeoffs when it gets to be too much of this and too little of that.

"One final point. Your model should change during your retirement years toward conservatism, but very slowly."

Grandpa reached into his filing cabinet and pulled out, once again, another chart. "Here, Jamie. This shows our six categories condensed into three basic components as a guide for a retired person."

Changes in Three Components of Retirement Portfolio

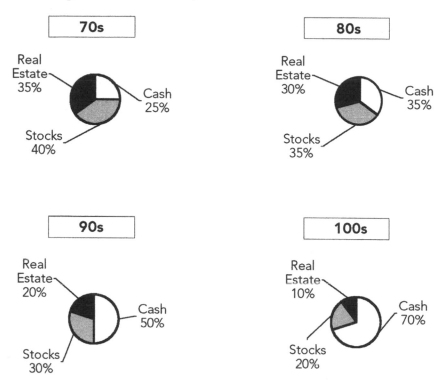

"Jamie, in my lectures, I stress the importance of avoiding any changes in the portfolio mix prior to retirement. A young person's investment portfolio is usually not balanced for many different reasons, but by age 40, or thereabouts, it should show a proper mixture. Then it should stay about the same all the way into retirement.[4]

"Some people say that a good deal of success is good luck. In response, I always quote Louis Pasteur: 'Chance favors only the mind that is prepared.' So be prepared. Develop a model portfolio using asset allocation in percentages and then work toward accomplishing those percentages. You also might hire an expert in this area, if for no other reason than to get a second opinion."

"I'm glad I don't have to do that, Grandpa," Jamie said. "I have the best expert in the whole world right in front of me, and I sure can't complain about your fees, at least what you charge me."

Grandpa tried to stifle his proud grin.

Jamie continued. "Little did I know what was involved when I asked my question three sessions ago. But I do have one more question."

"Not another hard one, I hope," Grandpa said, frowning.

"My question is, why do you refer to your clients so often as friends?"

Grandpa's frown turned into a smile. "I can answer that with no difficulty," he said. "As a financial consultant, I must become familiar with every detail of a client's life. I must thoroughly know the hard facts—the numbers—as well as soft facts—their attitudes, beliefs, goals, comfort levels, and so on. My clients and I become very close. We have to. But it has to be a two-way street. It's important that they get to know me very well in order to understand why I may make specific recommendations. In this process, we become friends."

"Grandpa, you really are rich, and rich in more ways than just in money. I remember back to when you began to answer my question about being rich. One of the things you said was, 'We are rich when we have good friends to cheer our hearts.' If, when I grow up, I decide to become a financial consultant—in fact, whatever I decide to be—I want to be just like you. Thanks for the wisdom. I love you."

Grandpa sat back, picked up his cup of tea, cold by now, and tried as hard as he could to memorize this moment so he would remember it forever.

notes

1. Sir John Marks Templeton, founder of the Templeton Mutual Fund Group. Early in life, he began to tithe and to give his time unselfishly to philanthropic

causes. He has since established several foundations to advance spiritual development. Perhaps his best-known effort has been the establishment of the Templeton Prize for Progress in Religion. Given annually, the monetary value of this award now exceeds that of the Nobel Prizes. The international importance of this gift has been recognized by no less than England's Queen Elizabeth II, who knighted John Templeton in 1987 for his service to philanthropy. Sir John, as he is known, sold his interest in the Templeton Group and is now retired.

2. Leverage produces a magnification of rates of return that results from investing borrowed funds in addition to your own funds and can be used to purchase securities as well as other properties.

3. Current income tax laws also allow an investment interest expense deduction, other than for personal residence, up to the amount of investment income.

4. This refers to the percentages for the categories, not the individual instruments within any category. For example, if 25 percent of your investments are to be in stocks, you or your advisor may choose a mix of mutual funds offering growth, income, emerging companies, foreign companies, and so on. Not only might the percentages within this mix change as various circumstances change, but each fund might range (or change) from aggressive to conservative depending upon your attitude or age.

chapter 13

Time to Pay the Piper

Rocky and Sandy Rhoades find themselves ready to retire with a rather tidy amount of assets. They have always been cautious and played by the rules, and now they want to carefully employ the correct methods of using their retirement assets to create the income needed to maintain their desired standard of living.

So, as they had done many times over the years during which they amassed their nest egg, the Rocky and Sandy called their understanding and trusted financial advisor.

They made a wise decision. Tax laws, revenue rulings, revenue procedures, and the related court cases are all in a state of flux. What is true today may be only partially so tomorrow. And although the information provided in this chapter is correct as of the time it was written, do not make any firm decisions based on the data without first consulting a tax specialist, as the Rhoades couple did.

Most retirement assets are accumulated both outside of and within formal or legally defined retirement plans. Assets accumulated outside of retirement plans may incur some taxes when withdrawn, but usually only a part of the withdrawn amount is taxable since taxes have been paid on most, if not all, of these assets.

Let's suppose you have a mutual fund that you are maintaining for retirement. You have already paid taxes on the earnings you invested in the fund. You also might have paid taxes annually on part or all of the profits earned by and reinvested in the fund. When you withdraw assets from this fund, you do not owe taxes on the entire amount withdrawn since you have paid most or all of the taxes already.[1]

Assets in formal or legally defined retirement plans are taxed differently; when assets are withdrawn they are usually fully taxable.[2] This is because you have paid no tax on the earnings or principal, and each and every dollar you withdraw is taxable in the year of withdrawal. The tax laws regulating taxation of withdrawals from these retirement plans are special and complex, and proper attention to these laws is appropriate if your goal is to reduce taxes to the legal minimum.

Many pension plans, most profit-sharing plans, and all 401(k) and 403(b) plans allow participants to roll over the account balances into self-directed Individual Retirement Accounts under certain circumstances. Since such IRAs provide you more control and more opportunities for diversification, a rollover is the recommended procedure.

The remainder of this chapter will discuss only the many aspects of *required distributions* from IRAs that require you to pay taxes.

On January 11, 2001, a change of significant magnitude in the taxation of retirement-plan withdrawals became law. Prior to 2001, the Minimum Required Distribution (MRD) law was extremely complicated, so much so that few financial professionals understood all the intricacies. Uncle Sam, in one of his more generous moments, removed the vast majority of these difficult-to-understand provisions. Starting in 2001, the calculation of the MRD for IRAs and some of the other qualified plans has been simplified. The remaining qualified plans not included in

2001 are included in 2002. Further, on April 17, 2002, the Internal Revenue Service issued final rules which changed the distribution factors. Again, the IRS reduced the minimum distribution amount that is required to avoid penalties. The following key sections of the law are applicable.

Key Points: Required Minimum Distribution

1. Required Beginning Date. April 1 of the year following the calendar year in which the participant attains age 70$\frac{1}{2}$.

2. First Distribution Year. The year the participant attains age 70$\frac{1}{2}$. Even though the actual distribution may be delayed up to April of the following year, the amount is the same as if paid out without a delay.

3. Minimum Required Distribution (MRD). The minimum withdrawal necessary to avoid a 50 percent tax penalty.

4. Kinds of Distributions. There are two kinds of distributions that satisfy MRD rules: (1) Lump sum or a partial withdrawal equal to or in excess of MRD, and (2) Annuitization.

5. Distribution Amount. The distribution amount is based on the value on December 31 of the prior year divided by a factor specified by the IRS Table using the age on December 31 of the year of required distribution. Caution: The first distribution is based on the year the participant becomes 70$\frac{1}{2}$, even if this first distribution is postponed into the next year.

6. Beneficiary Designation. The beneficiary designation not only states who will receive the IRA account balance at the death of the participant, but of equal importance, it dictates the factor that is used to determine the minimum amount that must be distributed during the lifetime of the participant.

7. Spousal Beneficiary Option. A spousal beneficiary *always* has the option to roll over the death proceeds into his or her own IRA.

8. Multiple Beneficiaries. When there are multiple beneficiaries, the age of the oldest beneficiary is used to calculate life expectancies.

It is important to keep in mind that after age $59\frac{1}{2}$, the owner of an IRA can withdraw at any time any amount up to the entire value of the IRA without a tax penalty. Also note that starting at age $70\frac{1}{2}$, a certain portion must be withdrawn each year or a tax penalty will be imposed. This tax penalty currently is 50 percent of the amount that should have been withdrawn but was not.

Many retirees find themselves with sufficient resources early in retirement and do not need money from their IRA accounts. For them, the ability to postpone withdrawals without penalties is quite desirable. Therefore, the remainder of this chapter will concentrate on how to withdraw the minimum without incurring any tax penalty. Remember that after age $59\frac{1}{2}$ and regardless of the system chosen, you can withdraw any amount *over* the minimum without a tax penalty. So, let's explore the circumstances and best withdrawal methods for three retirees.

Mike and Mary Married

Mike is $70\frac{1}{2}$ this year, and his wife, Mary, is 68. At the end of last year, Mike's IRA account balance was \$270,000. Before his retirement, Mike had been an executive for a small manufacturing firm. After his retirement, Mike rolled over his 401(k) account into an IRA. Mary is the primary beneficiary and their children are the secondary beneficiaries. Mike's goal is to withdraw the minimum amount of money as long as possible, and he is working with his accountant, Sid Cipher, in an attempt to do just this.

Sid explained to Mike and Mary that the calculation of the Minimum Required Distribution is quite easy. He showed them the following table, used to calculate the amount.

Minimum Required Distributions

Age of Participant	Distribution Period	Age of Participant	Distribution Period
70	27.4	93	9.6
71	26.5	94	9.1
72	25.8	95	8.6
73	24.7	96	8.1
74	23.8	97	7.6
75	22.9	98	7.1
76	22.0	99	6.7
77	21.2	100	6.3
78	20.3	101	5.9
79	19.5	102	5.5
80	18.7	103	5.2
81	17.9	104	4.9
82	17.1	105	4.5
83	16.3	106	4.2
84	15.5	107	3.9
85	14.8	108	3.7
86	14.1	109	3.4
87	13.4	110	3.1
88	12.7	111	2.9
89	12.0	112	2.6
90	11.4	113	2.4
91	10.8	114	2.1
92	10.2	115 and older	1.9

time to pay the piper

"The age we select on the table," Sid said, "will be Mike's actual age as of the *end* of the year he becomes age 70½. Since Mike was born on May 18, the calculation factor, 27.4, is based on age 70. Had Mike been born in the second half of the preceding year, he would become 70½ this year, but he would also become age 71 by the end of this year. Then we would have to use the factor for age 71, which is 26.5. The calculation is simple to make."

Sid picked up his calculator, entered some numbers, and wrote down what he did to show to Mike and Mary.

$270,000 ÷ 27.4 = $9,854.02

"You always round up the result," Sid said. "It is also important to remember the 27.4 is a *factor*, not a *percent*. If you are interested in calculating the percent, you divide $9,854.02 by $270,000 and find that the required withdrawal is 3.6 percent for this year."

Sid further explained that Mike's selection of beneficiaries would also provide for the best tax control even after his death. If Mary survives Mike, she can roll over the IRA balance into her own IRA. If Mary dies before Mike, their children can continue withdrawals over the balance of their lives after Mike dies. This would allow for required taxation only on the amount paid out to them each year. This new feature in the tax law can be wonderful news for many families.

As Mike and Mary prepared to leave their accountant's office, Sid said, "Oh, there is one more important aspect to these deliberations. It is important that you not name your revocable living trust as primary *or* secondary beneficiary. Your attorney has wisely recommended that your trust be the owner or beneficiary of all your *other* assets, but to maintain the tax control we just discussed, Mary and the children need to be named directly as beneficiaries.

"Mike, there is one exception. You could have your attorney draft special language in a trust to allow for this beneficial tax control and then name your trust as beneficiary, but in your case, I don't believe it is necessary. In any case, it wouldn't be a bad idea to have a discussion with your attorney on this point."

William Widower

William was married for many years, but an accident claimed the life of his wife, Wilma, when she was only 60 years old. William has been a widower for ten years now.

This year William will be $70^1/_2$ years old. He has accumulated a sizable IRA account from a combination of sources: Wilma's 403(b), his own 401(k), and a lump sum distribution from his pension plan. The current value is $750,000.

William has three adult children. He never remarried, but he does have a companion, Wanda, who also has grown children. William and Wanda have been living together for over six years. They have no intention of ever getting married, and each wishes to leave his or her assets to their respective children. There is one problem with this: should William die first, Wanda would not have enough income to support her. They took their problem to William's attorney, Timothy Tort.

Timothy recommended that William use a special trust as beneficiary of his IRA account. At William's death, the trust would make a regular payment to Wanda, which along with the income Wanda receives from her own assets would provide the desired standard of living. When Wanda dies, the income would be paid to William's children.

William could have named Wanda directly as primary beneficiary instead of going through a trust, but that would not guarantee that the balance of the account at Wanda's death would go to William's children. Or William could have named his children as primary beneficiary, but that would not guarantee that his desire to assist Wanda would be carried out. Therefore, William agreed with his attorney that this special trust appears to be the best arrangement.

If William and Wanda ever decide to get married, William could create an IRA Marital QTIP Trust. This trust would accomplish the same results with one additional advantage: rather than the IRA being subject to Federal Estate Tax at William's death, this tax would be postponed until after the death of Wanda.

Steve and Alice: A September–April Marriage

Steve and Alice have $1,000,000 in their IRA. This year Steve will become 70$\frac{1}{2}$, while Alice is only 50 years old. They are about to celebrate thirty years of this September–April marriage. Steve and Alice have raised three children. When they sat down with their financial advisor, Ivan Integrity, they learned of an unexpected benefit they were entitled to because of the difference in their ages—a benefit that comes with a new set of complications.

Ivan explained the procedure for calculating the Minimum Required Distribution—the same as that used for Mike and Mary in our first example—although a different government distribution table is used.

"Since your age spread is more than ten years," Ivan said, "we are required to use a table that is a bit more complicated. Actually, it produces a factor much higher than if your age difference were ten years or less. If your ages were within a ten-year spread, the required withdrawal from your million-dollar IRA would be $1,000,000 divided by 27.4, or $36,497. But the factor for your first withdrawal using ages 70 and 50 is 35.1. So, your required withdrawal this year is $1,000,000 divided by 35.1, or $28,490. This means you can take out $8,007 less than if Steve were ten years younger or Alice ten years older.

"Of course, if you need or want more, there is no limit to how much of the $1,000,000 you can withdraw. The lesser withdrawal amount gives you the advantage of paying less income tax. Plus, it gives you one other very important nontax benefit."

Ivan looked at Steve and said, "Steve, I'm sure this is a surprise to you, but the mortality tables say that Alice will outlive you."

"Those tables don't apply to me," Steve countered. "I'm going to live forever."

Steve winked at Alice and continued. "Alice and I have faced that issue and, of course, we are fully aware that she won't have to put up with me forever. So what's this added benefit, Ivan?"

"The benefit," Ivan said, "is that with lower required distributions, when you do die, Steve, there will be more money to help fund Alice's longer life expectancy." They all agreed this was indeed a good benefit.

Other Issues

There are not enough pages in any book to offer case studies to fit the circumstances of each and every person's retirement plans. But having read the case studies just presented, you now are more knowledgeable than you were before, and all such knowledge gives you greater power over your future.

There still are two other important topics that every owner of an IRA should know something about. One is *annuitization*, and the other is *taxation at the death of an IRA owner*.

Annuitization. An annuity is the perfect vehicle for retirement income—for providing money forever. It creates a stream of income that lasts as long as you do, or you and a beneficiary. You can transfer all or any portion of your IRA into an immediate annuity. The insurance company offering the annuity makes all of the calculations and offers a selection of options from which you can choose.

The good points of an immediate annuity include the fact that the required calculations need to be made only once. Once that is done, each and every month, regardless of the option chosen, you receive a check that is in compliance with the Minimum Required Distribution rules. This assures you of being penalty-free for life.

Another benefit of annuities is that you have the option to invest the account assets in stock market growth portfolios.

Historically, such portfolios have earned at a rate greater over long periods of time than what is needed to offset inflation.

A word of caution: too many IRA owners are tempted to choose a fixed annuity with a level payout. As we have demonstrated, inflation over time always destroys the purchasing power of a level stream of income. Before choosing any options offered to you, consider the effects not only at the time of retirement but several years into retirement, as well.

Taxation at the Death of an IRA Owner. It is not possible to include in this book the massive subject of estate planning. I would be remiss, however, if I did not mention the tax implications of IRAs inherited by anyone other than a spouse. Such taxes include both income and Federal Estate Taxes.

With the Federal Estate Tax starting at 41 percent effective in 2002, even a moderately wealthy person can be subject to a sizable death tax. However, when someone other than the spouse inherits an IRA balance, not only are the funds subject to Federal Estate Tax but to income tax, as well. This combination could produce an extremely high total tax. Uncle Sam figures that you should have used up these funds while you were still alive, and if you did not, then Uncle becomes a significant beneficiary.

You do have options, regardless of your current age. See your financial advisor, accountant, and attorney to discuss these important issues.

notes

1. Since the law does not require you to take withdrawals from investments outside of formal retirement plans, these amounts of tax are based on standard income tax law. Because such laws are constantly subject to change, it would be imprudent to discuss them in this book.

2. An exception is the Roth IRA. With certain qualifications, withdrawals from Roth IRAs are free of all income tax.

chapter 14

Assess Your Risk Tolerance

Five-year-old Ima Kidd walks into her parents' bedroom closet to play grownup using mommy's hats and shoes. A gust of wind blows the closet door shut and plunges Ima into total darkness. A moment ago the closet filled Ima's mind with unlimited possibilities for fun. Now it fills her mind with absolute terror.

What changed? It was not the content of the closet that changed, but rather Ima's perception of it. When she had enough light to see, she was happy. When she did not have enough light to see, she was scared.

In investing, too, perception makes all the difference. In this case, it is knowledge, not light, that differentiates what is real from what is perceived to be real.

Consider another example. Suppose when you were young, you began to hear stories about how Uncle Ferdinand lost all of his money in the stock market. With Uncle Ferdinand stories ringing in your head, you probably would be reluctant to invest much, if anything, in the market.

Now let's change your childhood experience. Suppose at a very young age you began to hear stories about how Aunt Isabella became unbelievably wealthy by investing her money in the stock market. With Aunt Isabella stories bouncing around inside your cranium, you may be talked into just about any investment that has something to do with stocks.

The only important difference between these two cases is not the stock market, but your perception of it. Many people who have either a very low or a very high tolerance for taking financial risks are like Ima Kidd in that dark closet. Their information about investing may be no more valuable than Uncle Ferdinand or Aunt Isabella stories. By opening the closet door to allow in the light of information about how investments work, they will acquire a tolerance level that will let them develop a well-diversified investment portfolio appropriate to their wants, needs, and resources.

The stock market can be downright mortifying for people who have little or no knowledge of just what it is, how it operates, and what can be done to offset much of the risk. Many of us have read or seen accounts of investors jumping out of tall buildings during the crash of 1929. Some of us have family legends often repeated over Thanksgiving dinners of how Uncle Clyde "lost his shirt gambling in the stock market." Others repeat the story about how the little old lady trusted her stockbroker only to have him churn[1] her account until all her money was out of her stock portfolio and into the personal account of her broker.

Unfortunately, such stories are occasionally true. People did commit suicide over the 1929 crash, and there are some unscrupulous promoters in the stock-brokerage business. People who could afford to stay the course through the 1930s, however, accumulated considerable wealth, and what business or profession does not have its share of crooks or quacks?

If you believe you are one of those with a low risk-taking tolerance, perhaps you should spend some time learning how investments really work. If you are not yet surfing the Net, then look to libraries. Most local libraries have a wealth of information on every type of investment invented. There also should be workshops and seminars in your area that provide an extensive education in investments and investment strategies. There also are many knowledgeable financial advisors ready to serve you.

When it comes to selecting a seminar or financial advisor, you should give serious consideration to the qualifications of the instructor or advisor. Look for designations such as CLU for Chartered Life Underwriter, ChFC for Chartered Financial Consultant, and CFP for Certified Financial Planner. These financial professionals earn the right to use these initials by successfully completing a number of specified courses at the college or university level.

Furthermore, each of these designated professionals agrees to abide by a code of ethics adopted by the organization. For example, the Certified Financial Planner Board of Standards governs financial planners with a CFP license and requires a strict code of conduct regarding integrity, objectivity, competence, fairness, confidentiality, professionalism, and diligence. The Society of Financial Service Professionals[2] requires similar responsibilities to the public and clients. If you take care to choose a qualified professional as your teacher or advisor, you take a giant step toward reducing your risk—perceived or real.

Risk is the possibility of suffering harm or loss. For many people, risk is a four-letter word for something that should be avoided at all costs. There are people who will drive hours or days to reach a destination rather than risk flying, totally ignoring that their probability of being in a fatal accident is much greater when traveling by car than by plane. There even are people who are so averse to risk that they seldom leave their homes, even though the greatest number of accidents occur in the home.

These people's irrational reactions—whatever the cause—may be depriving them of much pleasure. For them, the closet door is closed and they either refuse or are unable to open it to let in some light. No life is without risk. The best anyone can do is to not take a risk unnecessarily and to attempt to minimize any risk that is necessary to take.

Just as living is not without risks, so too is investing. No matter where you place your money, you place it at risk. Consider where the most risk-averse people place their money for safekeeping—in their local bank. Of course you know about the bank failures during the Great Depression, but that's history. Since then, the government has enacted laws to protect bank deposits up to a specified amount. This amount has increased gradually over the years in banks insured by the Federal Deposit Insurance Corporation (FDIC). But the real risk of keeping your money in savings investments, including CDs and interest-paying savings and checking accounts, is the loss of purchasing power.

Suppose last week you bought a CD at your local bank. They told you what rate of return you would earn, which by law they had to. When the CD matures, you expect to have earned whatever money this rate of your investment represents. And you will. The problem is that you are overlooking the real question. Are you further ahead on the day the CD matures than on the day you invested in the CD? It is a question you should ask regarding any of your investments.

The "real" rate of return on CDs is calculated by reducing the stated (nominal) rate by inflation and taxation. Here is how to make the calculations. First, determine your taxation of the gross rate of return. Second, determine how inflation affects the value of your account after adding the net interest (amount of interest minus income tax). The table on the facing page shows some examples assuming the CD was held for one full year.

In three of the six years noted, there was a loss in the purchasing power of the money invested. In other words, if you had bought a CD in any of these years and held for one year, you would have been able to buy less with the principal plus interest, minus taxation and inflation, than you would have before you invested. In the other three years you would have had a slight increase. In 1985, your increase in purchasing power would have been 1.5 percent. And should your income tax bracket be higher than the 28 percent used in the examples, you could have experienced a substantial loss of purchasing power.

These figures don't mean that you should rush out and dispose of any savings investments you have. There are many other reasons to have this type of accumulation. The examples

Result of $1,000 Invested in 6-month CDs After Federal Income Tax (28% assumed) and Inflation (actual rate)

Year	CD Rate	Net Rate After 28% Income Tax	Net Interest Added to $1,000	Inflation Rate	Year-End Net Purchasing Power of $1,000
1975	6.41%	4.6%	$1,046	7.0%	$973
1980	12.00%	8.6%	$1,086	12.4%	$951
1985	7.68%	5.5%	$1,055	3.8%	$1,015
1990	8.11%	5.8%	$1,058	6.1%	$993
1995	5.20%	3.7%	$1,037	2.5%	$1,011
2000	6.64%	4.8%	$1,048	3.4%	$1,012

do tell you that loss of purchasing power is an important risk involved in what many perceive to be a "safe" investment.

When it comes to the stock market, volatility is one risk that can rattle the cages of people who abhor change. The stock market often resembles a scary roller-coaster ride. By understanding how this up-and-down movement is leveled out over time, most people take a calmer view and happily invest some of their money in the market.

Some notable aberrations can be found when you research the history of the stock market. On October 19, 1987, the market fell 22.6 percent. The decline is even worse if you back up a bit and look at the market from August 25 through October 19 of that year. During this period the Dow Jones Industrial Average dropped from 2722 to 1738, a precipitous fall of nearly 36 percent. But you gain perspective when you look at longer periods of time, which make October 1987 seem a mere hiccup, not a fatal disease.

Consider a study made by Haas Financial Services of twenty-year periods in the market beginning in 1926 and ending in 2000. There are fifty-six such periods. The S&P 500 is used to represent the stock market in this study.

assess your risk tolerance

20-Year Periods S&P 500

Period	Aver. Annual Rate of Return	Period	Aver. Annual Rate of Return
1926–1945	7.14%	1954–1973	10.86%
1927–1946	6.08%	1955–1974	6.88%
1928–1947	4.70%	1956–1975	7.11%
1929–1948	3.09%	1957–1976	7.91%
1930–1949	4.44%	1958–1977	8.12%
1931–1950	7.42%	1959–1978	6.53%
1932–1951	1.70%	1960–1979	6.83%
1933–1952	13.14%	1961–1980	8.31%
1934–1953	10.66%	1962–1981	6.76%
1935–1954	13.11%	1963–1982	8.29%
1936–1955	12.46%	1964–1983	8.28%
1937–1956	11.18%	1965–1984	7.78%
1938–1957	12.95%	1966–1985	8.66%
1939–1958	13.46%	1967–1986	10.17%
1940–1959	14.13%	1968–1987	9.27%
1941–1960	14.75%	1969–1988	9.54%
1942–1961	6.84%	1970–1989	11.54%
1943–1962	15.24%	1971–1990	11.14%
1944–1963	15.10%	1972–1991	11.88%
1945–1964	14.94%	1973–1992	11.33%
1946–1965	13.83%	1974–1993	12.75%
1947–1966	13.73%	1975–1994	14.57%
1948–1967	14.64%	1976–1995	14.58%
1949–1968	14.94%	1977–1996	14.55%
1950–1969	13.45%	1978–1997	16.65%
1951–1970	12.11%	1979–1998	17.75%
1952–1971	11.66%	1980–1999	17.88%
1953–1972	11.69%	1981–2000	15.68%

Fifty-Six 20-Year Periods
1926–2000

S&P 500 Aver. Total Return Range	Number of Periods	Percent of Total
3.00–3.99%	1	1.82%
4.00–4.99%	2	3.64%
5.00–5.99%	0	0.00%
6.00–6.99%	5	9.09%
7.00–7.99%	5	9.09%
8.00–8.99%	5	9.09%
9.00–9.99%	2	3.64%
10.00–10.99%	3	5.45%
11.00–11.99%	8	12.73%
12.00–12.99%	4	7.27%
13.00–13.99%	6	10.91%
14.00–14.99%	8	14.55%
15.00–15.99%	3	5.45%
16.00–16.99%	2	3.64%
17.00–17.99%	2	3.64%

assess your risk tolerance

The most interesting result of this study is that there was not a single negative return in any of the fifty-six periods. The lowest average annual return was 3.09 percent for the twenty-year period from 1929 through 1948 that included the Great Depression. The highest average annual return was 17.9 percent during the period from 1980 through 1999.

The median, or middle average, annual rate of return for the twenty-year periods falls between 11 and 11.99 percent. This means that at least half of the periods yielded annual returns greater than 11 percent. And nearly 90 percent of the periods yielded annual returns between 6 and 16 percent. The average annual return for all the years beginning with 1926 and ending with 2000 was 11.3 percent.

If you want to think about a real roller-coaster dip, the annual rate of return in 1931 was -43.4 percent—that's *minus* 43.4 percent—but just two years later in 1933, the annual rate of return was 54 percent—that's *plus* 54 percent.

This shows how volatile the stock market can be. It also shows that over long periods of time the market is less volatile, and for twenty-year periods the market has not yielded a loss to date.

Michael Roszkowski, Ph.D., formerly with The American College in Bryn Mawr, Pennsylvania, is a specialist in the study of risk tolerance. He states, "To properly evaluate a person's risk tolerance, you need to ask 21 questions in each of four areas." In my practice, I use a questionnaire that asks only one question in each of the four areas.[3] Obviously, my short survey cannot be considered a full psychological evaluation, but over many years of using the four-question questionnaire I am able to establish a very strong correlation between my client's score on the questionnaire and his or her real comfort level in investments. I recommend that you respond honestly to these four questions (shown on the following two pages) and then evaluate your responses using a self-evaluation form found in Appendix 4. Remember, there are no right or wrong answers.

Financial Attitude Questionnaire

Question 1 asks you to circle 1, 2, or 3 for each of ten different investment vehicles. If you feel uncomfortable, then circle 1; if you feel comfortable, then circle 3; and if you feel neither one way nor the other, then circle 2. If you are not familiar with any of the investments listed, refer to Chapter 11 for further information. Your response should be based on "how you feel" about each investment vehicle, not on whether you have invested or plan to invest in it.

1. Rate the following methods of saving and investing.

	Uncomfortable		Comfortable
Savings Account	1	2	3
Cash Value of Life Insurance	1	2	3
Government Bonds	1	2	3
Corporate Bonds	1	2	3
Tax Exempt Bonds	1	2	3
Mutual Funds (Stocks)	1	2	3
Variable Annuities (Stocks)	1	2	3
Common Stocks	1	2	3
Real Estate	1	2	3
Tax Shelters (oil, cattle, etc.)	1	2	3

Question 2 deals with a hypothetical investment that will last three years. It is all over after three years. Circle Yes or No for each a, b, and c.

2. Would you be willing to invest in a three-year investment that

a)   had a 90% chance of a 100% gain
      and a 10% chance of a 50% loss   Yes   No

b)   had a 90% chance of a 50% gain
      and a 10% chance of a 25% loss   Yes   No

c)   had a 90% chance of a 25% gain
      and a 10% chance of a 10% loss   Yes   No

Question 3 is in two parts. If you answer No to the first part, then do not respond to the second part. If you answer Yes to the first part, then state in the second part the portion of your assets you would be willing to allocate.

3. In the handling of your finances, would you
be willing to take above-average risks in
order to seek greater growth with some or
all of your investable funds?   Yes   No

If Yes, indicate what percent of your
investable funds you would be willing
to place in investments of
above-average risk.   _____ Percent

Question 4 asks you to prioritize a list of important items. You are to put a 5 on the most important item, a 4 on the next most important item, etc. You will give no response to two items.

4. Choose five items you consider more important than the two remaining items. Then rank the items in order of importance. Write 5 before the most important, 4 before the next most important, then 3, then 2, and then 1.

a)   _____   Liquidity (availability)
b)   _____   Current Income from Investments
c)   _____   Future Income
d)   _____   Inflation Protection (assuring
                purchasing power)
e)   _____   Income Tax Deferral/Relief
f)   _____   Capital Growth
g)   _____   Safety of Principal

Now turn to Appendix 4 to evaluate your responses.

Attitude is such a personal matter that it is difficult to generalize. But attitudes are learned and, therefore, can be changed. If your current attitude is to freeze at the mere mention of the word *risk*, then this attitude is probably restricting your wealth accumulation. You feel like Ima Kidd did when the closet door slammed shut. You need to open the door and let in some light, some knowledge.

The accumulation and preservation of your money is at risk due to a lack of information on how investing works. If you are reading this chapter after reading Chapters 10, 11, and 12 on investments, you possibly feel more comfortable than you would had you not read these chapters. If you didn't read Chapters 10, 11, and 12, do so now, and if you still feel unreasonably uncomfortable at the sound of risk, explore the many other sources of information on investments available in your local library.

But first, accept the truth: There is no such thing as no risk! John R. Rowell, FCAS, MAAA, has stated:

"Retirees as individuals face the following financial risks:
- inflation risk
- interest rate risk
- security risk
- concentration risk
- currency risk
- economic risk
- political risk
- market risk
- longevity risk
- tax risk"

I don't want this rather long list of risks to scare you. But I do want you to understand four basic fundamentals of investing: (1) Every storage facility for your money has its own risk(s); (2) Seventy percent of all risk can be eliminated with diversification; (3) Attitudes are learned and can be unlearned; (4) The more you know about investing, the more comfortable you will be with your investments; the more comfortable you are with your investments, the more comfortable you will be the rest of your life.

notes

1. To churn is to buy and sell a client's securities frequently, especially in order to generate commissions.

2. The Society of Financial Service Professionals is composed of members who hold one or more of several designations: CLU, ChFC, CFP, et cetera.

3. The questionnaire was developed twenty-five years ago by Denis Raihall, PhD, CLU, of Westchester, Pennsylvania. He recently stated that he continues to use the questionnaire with extremely reliable results.

chapter 15

Stay Healthy
and Enjoy Your Wealth

A soft breeze wafts off the ocean on a bright sunny morning as Gary and Golda Golfer approach the first tee at the Paradise Golf Club. Golda drives the golf ball straight down the fairway. So does Gary. They put their clubs back in their bags and walk down the fairway toward the green.

For Gary and Golda, it truly is the best of all possible worlds. It has been ten years since they retired at the age of 65. Now, at the age of 75, they still have the health to play golf and the money to be members of a golf club. Take away their health or their wealth, however, and their wonderful world would instantly crumble.

Ask any retiree you know. You will find that each has two main concerns: money and health. The principles and practices discussed so far in this book will help you avoid running out of money in your retirement years. Now let's look at factors that affect your health, particularly since your lifestyle affects how long you will live and the amount of retirement money you will need.

Based on all the evidence, people in this country are living longer today than at any time in history. This includes you! But it's likely that just living longer is not your goal. You want the later years of your life to be quality ones—years in which you can enjoy the fruits of your labor.

I am a financial consultant, not a nutritionist or a medical specialist. So I readily admit that the best health advice I am qualified to give is to tell you to see your doctor on a regular basis, at least annually, and attend to his or her recommendations. With that said, there are some aspects of your lifestyle that you might consider adjusting in order to experience better living between these visits to your doctor.

The first important lifestyle category is exercise. I was in my late forties before I ever considered doing any exercise outside my usual activities of making a living. Participating in sports was something that other people spent a lot of time doing. That time was never available to me because I had other, more important things to do. So I thought.

It was in 1978 when I heard Kenneth Cooper, M.D., discuss aerobics and the importance of adequate cardiovascular activities. I felt that, at the young age of 48, I was in good enough shape to easily jog a mile or more. I was surprised to discover that I couldn't jog for more than three minutes, the time required to cover less than two-tenths of a mile. I tried again and again on several occasions, but three minutes was my limit.

I was sufficiently upset with my condition to buy Dr. Cooper's book on aerobics and follow his plan to the letter. His plan allowed me to slowly build up my stamina to the point where I was jogging at least three days a week, usually three miles each day. I did this for many years. Today, I walk briskly six days a week for an average of fifty minutes each day.

I know you are not interested in my personal history, but I cannot help but believe that, if I had been doing nothing about exercise, you possibly are doing nothing about it as well. Too many people think they are taking care of their bodies when, in fact, they are doing more damage than good to their most important muscle—the heart. The good news is that exercise doesn't have to take that much time and it doesn't have to cost you a dime.

The Cooper Clinic in Dallas, Texas, claims that even a simple activity like walking will suffice. Walking forty-five minutes a day, five days a week, will go far toward bringing your cholesterol level down and keeping it in balance. At the same time, a daily walk will eliminate many of those other ailments you may have been complaining about. And if you say you simply cannot find forty-five minutes a day for yourself, then you do not place a very high value on your being.

Food is the second important lifestyle category you should be concerned with. Do you really pay attention to the type of food you eat and how much you consume? Should you consider changing your diet? I personally believe that the best diet is a change for life and not just a temporary modification of improper consumption.

Most experts agree that the key concepts in dieting are balance and moderation. There are a number of reliable guides that outline what a diet should be for the average person. These range from the rather specific daily dietary allowances recommended by the Food and Nutrition Board of the National Academy of Sciences to the more general Food Guide Pyramid, which fits four food groups into a triangle in which those at the base should be eaten more frequently than those at the top. Keep in mind that all such diet guides are general, and specific needs will vary from individual to individual. Only a trained professional, such as a doctor or dietitian, should prescribe a specific diet for you.

Many people today are concerned with their cholesterol level. To keep cholesterol in check they constantly seek low-fat or fat-free foods. Of course, the body does need to ingest some fat to function properly, but problems arise when too much fat is ingested. What is too much? It can vary from individual to individual, but somewhere between 25 and 30 grams of fat per day should keep your cholesterol at a proper level. Naturally, if your blood tests indicate you have too much cholesterol, your doctor may recommend a different regimen that may include medications in addition to low-fat foods.

It is easy to manage your fat consumption once you learn

the fat content of the foods you eat. And learning this is easy. Simply get a guide such as the book *The Fat Counter* by Annette B. Natow and Jo-Ann Heslin. Then each day for three weeks, write down in a column everything you put into your stomach. In a second column, write down the number of grams of fat for each food item. When you get to 30 grams, stop eating all food that has any fat in it for the rest of that day.

I know that you will get hungry before the day is over if you consume all 30 grams of fat at breakfast, and it is not all that difficult to blow your daily allowance on the first meal.

Improper Breakfast	Fat Content
2 fried eggs	14 grams
3 fried strips of bacon	12 grams
1 cup of whole milk	8 grams
2 slices of toast with 1 pat of butter	6 grams
Total	40 grams

After some practice, it will soon become just as easy to have an excellent, tasty breakfast and still put barely a dent in your daily fat allowance.

Proper Breakfast	Fat Content
$1/_2$ grapefruit	0 grams
1 bowl of nonfat cereal with 1 cup fresh berries	1 gram
1 bagel or 2 slices of toast with preserves	2 grams
1 cup of skim milk	0 grams
Total	3 grams

After you have spent some time learning how many grams of fat are in the foods you consume, attempt to reduce the total daily intake to 25 or even 20 grams, depending on your weight and cholesterol ratio.

In his book *Dare to Be 100*, Dr. Walter M. Bortz II states, "The Prudent Diet says: Reduce the diet fat load. Choose lean meats. Use more poultry, fish. Remove visible fat (e.g., skin from chicken). Broil/bake; don't fry. Replace meat with vegetables. Use low-fat/no-fat milk and cheese. Watch the dressing, dips, popcorn butter."

Dr. Bortz asks the question, "What is the right recipe for living to 100?" The answer he supplies is, " . . . eat a varied diet, and the more varied the better, because keeping the choices plentiful ensures balanced nutrition of high quality."

Another book worth your attention is *The Good News About Nutrition, Exercise, and Weight Control*, by Dr. Fred W. Stransky. One of the chapters has the intriguing title, "How to Live to be 100 (and Why You Should Want To): Ten Steps to a Longer, Better Life."

Learn the amount of fat in the foods you eat and limit the total on a daily basis, and over time you will gravitate toward your proper weight. It is very difficult to consume too many calories eating low- or zero-fat foods, giving you the bonus of not having to skimp on your total intake of food.

As mentioned before, exercise is important to maintaining a proper cholesterol balance. You did notice, didn't you, that Gary and Golda Golfer walked down the fairway. They didn't waddle over to the golf cart to be hauled around like so much freight. Most people are able to maintain a high-quality lifestyle if they burn 2,000 calories per week from exercise.

Proper nutrition without proper exercise will not do it. A close friend of mine, let's call him Sonny, was one hundred pounds overweight. He went on a low-fat diet and used a treadmill and a stairclimber six days a week for forty-five minutes each day. Lo and behold, not only did Sonny lose his one hundred extra pounds, he kept them off by continuing his exercise program.

A few years later, during one of his routine visits to the doctor, Sonny was told that he must undergo a very serious operation. The doctor advised that to prepare for it, Sonny should stop his exercise program for one month. My friend followed his doctor's advice and stopped his exercising but continued his low-fat diet, and he gained ten pounds. His doctor, for reasons unrelated to Sonny's weight increase, postponed the operation for another month. Sonny continued his low-fat diet but still did no exercises. He gained another ten pounds. Finally, he underwent his operation, which, I am pleased to report, was a success.

A short time after the operation, Sonny returned to his daily exercise regimen and continued his low-fat diet, and he lost the excess weight. Of course, this is no scientific experiment, but it does lend support to the healthful benefits of combining a regular exercise program with a low-fat diet.

The third and fourth lifestyle categories are smoking and alcohol. I travel extensively both in the United States and around the world. The number of smokers in the United States has been cut in half, but this is not so in other countries. I have heard medical people say that smoking is directly or indirectly responsible for over 50 percent of all deaths. The death certificate might state that the cause of death was cancer or stroke or whatever, but the major contributor was smoking. So if you smoke, STOP! It won't be easy. I know this from my friends who have quit. But it will be easier than it used to be because there now are a variety of effective methods and products to help one stop. If you smoke, talk to your doctor about the help that is available to you.

"Cigarette smoking is under severe indictment as the single most easily identified destructive behavior," Dr. Bortz writes. "To me, smoking cigarettes is like driving through a blinking red light. It gives no warning of its impact until it is too late."

He also writes, "Alcohol comes in second to cigarettes as

an addictive villain. Twenty percent of diseases can claim a sub-stantial alcohol component."

You may read conflicting reports about alcohol. Some studies show that alcohol in moderation can be good for some people. Other people cannot tolerate any amount of alcohol. When there is an *excessive* use of alcohol, however, there are no conflicting reports. The person who drinks to excess should seek help before the practice takes its toll on the length and quality of life.

You should develop your own opinions on a healthy lifestyle based on the best current information available. Such information does not necessarily include what you learned as a child or what you hear from acquaintances who are not medical professionals. Reliable information is readily available from your doctor, from materials in your local library, and from data on the Internet. Always check the credentials of the source before accepting the advice you receive from magazines, books, and the Internet.

I spent a life-changing week at the Cooper Aerobics Clinic in Dallas, Texas, and I have continued to receive supervision at the Meadow Brook Health Enhancement Institute in Rochester, Michigan. Both of these reputable wellness organizations pre-scribe essentially the same thing: a low-fat diet with proper movement of the body. What a wellness organization can provide is a prescription tailor-made to your personal needs. You don't have to travel to Texas or Michigan to get such help. Often a serious conversation with your primary doctor will put you on the right track.

It also is important that you build a team of health special-ists. These people should be professionals who will take the time to learn about your body and then explain to you how it functions and what you can do to enhance your health. Remember, your body is the only vessel you will ever have. Sure, you might need a few additives or replacement parts now and then, but if you take care of your body, it will serve you well for a long time.

In *Age Wave: How the Most Important Trend of Our Time Will Change Our Future*, Ken Dychtwald, Ph.D., writes, "Eighty percent

of the health problems of older people are now thought to be preventable or postponable. What many of us call aging is instead a
lifestyle issue."

Since you have considerable control over your lifestyle, you
have considerable choice about how you will live and die. Make
the choice wisely and make it now.

chapter 16

The Adventures of Jamie and Grandpa, Part 4: The Coup de Grâce

"Help, Grandpa," exclaimed Jamie. "I have to write a term paper about money. You know, like when we were talking about investing and everything, but I want to take a broader approach."

"All right," Grandpa nodded, "providing it is not so broad that you exceed my area of knowledge."

"I don't think that's possible," Jamie said. "I wondered if you could give me an overview of the subjects or topics I should include in this paper, and maybe you could even give me a knock-out punch line or issue that would make the paper provocative enough for me to get an A."

"That's possible." Grandpa stroked his imaginary beard while contemplating the task. "But the subject of money is very extensive. Maybe you should limit it somehow."

"I agree. What I had in mind was, more or less, to list key items with brief explanations, and then conclude with whatever you feel is of major importance. Maybe even take a look at what might happen in the future."

"Well, it seems that you have already given quite a bit of thought to this project, haven't you?"

"Yes," Jamie said, smiling sheepishly. "But there is a small problem. I waited until the last minute and, well, I only have the weekend to get it done."

Grandpa slowly shook his head, recalling but not revealing how many times over the years he had done the same thing. "Well then, I guess we should get started."

"I already have," Jamie said, handing a pad of paper to Grandpa. The first page was blank except for a title centered at the top of the page: *Money Forever.*

"And I assume I am to fill in the blanks," chuckled Grandpa. "Suppose we discuss major items and you add your own brief explanations later. I know you have a keen memory, but take notes anyway. They will help you fill in the blanks later." Jamie nodded and took back the paper. Grandpa cautioned, "Now to get done, I'll move rather fast. Just stop me or interrupt if you have questions.

"I'd start with a brief history of the importance of two key topics. The first is the insidious nature of inflation. The second is the continuing increase in how long we are living."

Jamie interrupted. "Tell me a little about each."

"Jamie, the USA has had inflation every year since 1955 [see Chapters 1, 3, and 6]. Back in the decade of the 1930s, on the other hand, one-half of the years were deflationary. You know I give a lot of speeches each year to a lot of groups of people. I often ask facetiously whether there is anyone in the audience who believes that we will never have another year of inflation. Of course, I never see a hand raised. So put inflation at the top of your list. You might want to include a graph like this one to illustrate how long-term inflation can really destroy the purchasing power of your money."

Grandpa reached into his desk drawer, pulled out a piece of paper, and passed it to Jamie, who studied it for a minute.

Time-Adjusted Purchasing Power

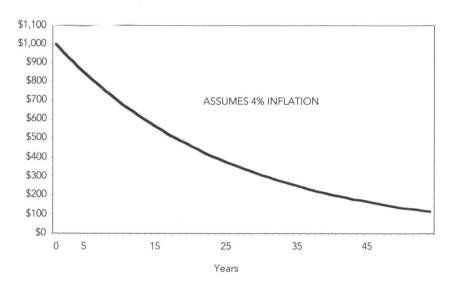

"Okay," Jamie said, looking up, "what's next?"

"Next," Grandpa continued, "is life expectancy and how it continues to increase [see Chapter 2]. As you and I have discussed many times, people are living longer than ever before, and it seems that our potential for living to be 100 years old increases every day. It is important for those who plan for retirement to consider this fact carefully, because it means that more retirement income will be needed to cover these additional years.

"Next in order of importance is an understanding of the different sources of money for retirees [see Chapter 7]. The three primary sources are Social Security, employer pension plans, and personal wealth accumulation. Of these three sources, a retiree's personal accumulated assets is very quickly becoming the most important. You might want to place some emphasis here on the importance of starting early in life to save and invest money, but be sure to say that it is never too late.

"Actually, I suppose we should consider a fourth source of money in retirement, and this is working to earn money. Some people choose to work well into the normal retirement ages because they just like what they are doing. My feelings are that if this is someone's choice, then it's great, but if someone has to work in his or her retirement years because there is insufficient income for the desired standard of living, then it's really a shame.

"Jamie, I guess you just can't emphasize enough the importance of starting to accumulate wealth as early in life as possible."

Jamie looked up from taking notes and said with great sincerity, "Grandpa, I certainly have learned that lesson. I just wish that everybody could have the benefit of your wisdom."

"Jamie," Grandpa continued, "when I work with people on their retirement plans, I have found that it is of extreme importance to emphasize that they should plan on inflation continuing for most of their future years, and they should plan to make their money last until age 100, at least.

"To help people with the calculation of how much future income they will need and how this need will be met, I've developed a computer program called Retirement Cash Flow Analysis [see Chapter 9]. It's the same one I gave you last year. Did you ever use it?"

"No, not yet," Jamie answered, "but it looks like I'm going to use it this weekend."

"You may not have time this weekend, but if you can squeeze it in, you could run a hypothetical illustration to be included in your report."

"What a great idea, Grandpa. I'll really try to get it in. Now, what's next?"

"Next on your list should be the development of a Cash Management Statement [see Chapters 4 and 5]. If you remember a long time ago, when you did the paper on money management, you created a hypothetical listing of expenses for a make-believe couple. Then you pretended that they were about to retire, and you tried to guess how their itemized expenses would be different in retirement."

Jamie laughed. "Yes, I remember, and I also remember how

far off I was when you reviewed my guesses. But you did say how good I was understanding the logic behind the differences in the amounts of money that would be paid out of the various pension plan options." [See Chapter 8.]

"Right, Jamie, and you have just come up with the next item on your list of topics for your term paper. Maybe you really don't need my help after all."

"No way, Grandpa."

"Okay," Grandpa continued, "the next topic should be about the storage categories for money. Do you remember the three long sessions we had on those?" [See Chapters 10, 11, and 12.]

"Yes, I do," Jamie said. "Actually, after each session, I wrote down as much as I could remember. It was obvious that becoming wealthy is much more complicated than I thought. I'm glad I did make those notes, not only because I'm still serious about becoming wealthy, but also because I can use the information to write my report this weekend."

"Good, Jamie. Now, your report could also include a few miscellaneous topics such as risk tolerance, taxation of withdrawals from retirement plans, and how everyone needs to recognize the importance of the wealth-health equation." [See Chapters 2 and 15.]

"Great, Grandpa. Is that it?"

"No, you still need a coup de grâce."

"A what?"

"A coup de grâce," replied Grandpa. "A finishing stroke or decisive event. You said you needed one to earn an A."

"Oh, right," Jamie said. "So, what's the big finish?"

"I don't know if I have discussed this with you before," Grandpa said, suddenly very serious, "but I still get quite upset when I hear or read about someone giving advice on retirement money and using wrong or outdated information."

"What kind of wrong or outdated information?" Jamie asked.

"Too many financial advisors and financial writers are still telling it the way it was many, many years ago," Grandpa said. "What they are telling people was correct back in the 1930s, but it's no longer that way, and what they are saying is just plain wrong for today." Grandpa noticed that Jamie looked a little puzzled, so he took a different tack.

"Let's go back in history, back to the 1930s. Back then, we had years with deflation as well as years with inflation. People also had much shorter life expectancies. When President Roosevelt signed the first Social Security Act in 1935, his advisors told him, 'Mr. President, don't worry about the cost of this legislation, because these Social Security benefits don't begin until a person reaches age 65, and the average life expectancy is age 62. This legislation won't cost us anything.' " Jamie looked startled when Grandpa began to chuckle but then joined Grandpa in laughing out loud.

"Jamie, back then financial advisors concluded that "safety first" was the key to successfully managing a person's or family's retirement money. This was because they felt that, since life expectancy was so short, people would not have time to recover from a major drop in the stock market or real estate values. Now give the Devil his due. Back in the 1930s, they were in the middle of a severe economic crisis that followed the 1929 stock market crash. Many people wondered if they would live long enough to see a recovery.

"Back then, the theory was developed that as the date for retirement approached, wise investors should start to transfer their investments out of equity-type investments—stocks and real estate—and into fixed-dollar-type investments—savings accounts, bonds, CDs, and so forth. Some even advised investors to begin doing this quite a long time before retirement.

"That was not wrong advice back in the 1930s, Jamie, but that was then and this is now." He reached once again into his desk drawer and brought out another graph, which he handed to Jamie.

Conventional Wisdom

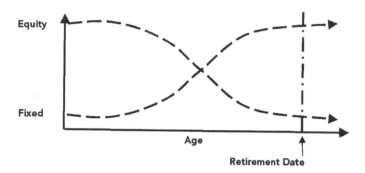

"When I saw this graph a few years ago in a new publication, I was appalled. To this day, I still get upset just talking about it. So, I studied the graph long and hard until I figured out a way to fix it."

"What did you do, Grandpa?"

"Well, Jamie, it's much like the feeling you have when someone tells you the answer to a riddle. You think, 'Why of course; it's obvious; why didn't I think of that?' Like most solutions, it is obvious after someone points it out to you."

"So, what was your solution?"

"Look at the graph again, Jamie. Do you see the vertical line for retirement?" Jamie nodded, and Grandpa went on. "Well, suppose you just move that line quite a bit to the left. Now what does the graph say?"

The New Wisdom

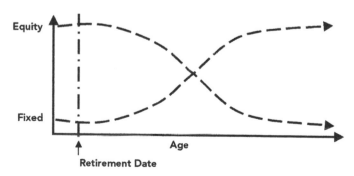

the coup de grâce

"Now it says one should begin to transfer investments out of equity types into fixed-income types long after one retires."

"Correct! Jamie, you might remember that, in our last discussion some time ago, I illustrated the investment portfolio adjustments that one should make throughout retirement like this." He handed Jamie another graph.

Changes in Three Components of Retirement Portfolio

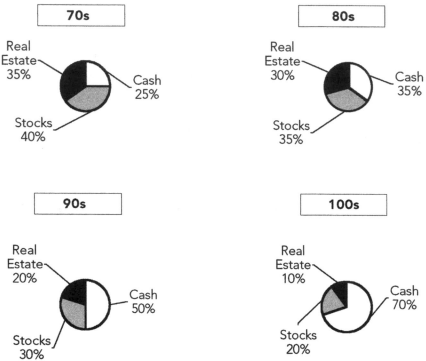

"This graph indicates that retirement money should be transferred *very slowly* to fixed-dollar-type investments. Note also that this transfer begins *after* retirement, *not before.*"

"Wow, Grandpa!" exclaimed Jamie. "This really is a coup de grâce. Wait until old Mr. Stodgy reads this. It's a guaranteed A."

"Well," said Grandpa as he arose from his chair behind the

oak desk that used to be his father's, "I don't know about the A, but I hope that you have learned an important lesson from this. What is best in the past is not always best in the present or for the future. You can be sure that by the time you retire, things will be different again."

"You sure have to be up-to-date all the time, don't you, Grandpa?"

"Just be like a mountain goat, Jamie. Be agile but sure-footed."

Jamie looked at Grandpa for a few moments and then said, "I want to be just like you, Grandpa."

Grandpa felt a lump forming in his throat. "If you decide to become a financial consultant, and you don't keep current with the changing times, I will come back and haunt you."

Jamie said nothing and Grandpa began to wonder if he had said something wrong. Then Jamie reached out and hugged him. "With a Grandpa like you, I would welcome your haunting me forever. That way, I could always have your advice and love."

Much later, in fact far into that night, Grandma came into the den looking for Grandpa. When she saw him sitting in the dark behind the desk, she asked, "So, are you coming to bed?"

"Only if I can take the moment I am savoring with me," he replied.

Grandma smiled. "Then certainly, bring it along."

Appendices

Appendix 1
Cash Management Statement

Annual Expenditures: Fixed	Annual
Housing (Mortgage/Rent)	$ _____
Property Taxes	_____
House Upkeep/Repairs/Maintenance	_____
Utilities and Telephone	_____
Food/Groceries	_____
Clothing & Cleaning	_____
Income Taxes and Social Security Taxes	_____
Debt Payment	_____
Transportation (Auto/Commuting)	_____
Auto, Home, and Liability Insurance	_____
Medical/Dental/Drugs/Health Insurance	_____
Disability Income Insurance	_____
Life Insurance	_____
Education Expenses	_____
Total Fixed Expenditures	$ _____

Annual Expenditures: Discretionary	
Vacation/Travel	$ _____
Recreation/Entertainment	_____
Contributions	_____
Gifts	_____
Household Furnishings	_____
Education Fund	_____
Personal Care	_____
Other	_____
Total Discretionary Expenditures	$ _____
Total Annual Expenditures	$ _____
Estimated Income	$ _____

Appendix 2
Social Security Retirement Age

Year of Birth	Full Retirement Age	Year Age 62	Age 62 Benefit as % of PIA★
1937 or earlier	65	1999 or earlier	80.0%
1938	65 and 2 months	2000	79.2%
1939	65 and 4 months	2001	78.3%
1940	65 and 6 months	2002	77.5%
1941	65 and 8 months	2003	76.7%
1942	65 and 10 months	2004	75.8%
1943–1954	66	2005–2016	75.0%
1955	66 and 2 months	2017	74.2%
1956	66 and 4 months	2018	73.3%
1957	66 and 6 months	2019	72.5%
1958	66 and 8 months	2020	71.7%
1959	66 and 10 months	2021	70.8%
1960 and later	67	2022 and after	70.0%

★*PIA is Primary Insurance Amount*

Appendix 3
Retirees Residence Feasibility Study

Proper Price of Residence(s)

$800,000 (Total Investment) x 0.25 = $200,000

Proper Mortgage Amount

$800,000	Total Investments
x 0.25	
$200,000	
-$300,000	Price of Residence(s)
$100,000	Amount of Mortgage

Proper Mortgage Payments

	Annual Payment		Monthly Payment
Maximum:			
$75,000(income) x 0.25 =	$18,750	÷ 12	$1,563
Ideal:			
$75,000(income) x 0.15 =	$11,250	÷ 12	$938

Considerations

Price of Residence(s)	$300,000	$200,000
Down Payment	-$200,000	-$200,000
Mortgage	$100,000	$0
Monthly Payment	$900	$0
(15 years @ 7%)		

Appendix 4
Evaluation Form: Financial Attitude Questionnaire
(Scores shown in italic)

1. Rate the following methods of saving and investing.

	UNCOMFORTABLE		COMFORTABLE
Savings Account	1	2	3
Cash Value of Life Insurance	1	2	3
Government Bonds	1	2	3
Corporate Bonds	1	2	3
Tax Exempt Bonds	1	2	3
Mutual Funds (Stocks)	1	2	3
Variable Annuities (Stocks)	1	2	3
Common Stocks	1	2	3
Real Estate	1	2	3
Tax Shelters (oil, cattle, etc.)	1	2	3

> *One point for each number 1 circled on first five categories;*
> *One point for each number 3 circled on last five categories.*

2. Would you be willing to invest in a three-year investment that
   a) had a 90% chance of a 100% gain
      and a 10% chance of a 50% loss   Yes *(3)*   No *(0)*

   b) had a 90% chance of a 50% gain
      and a 10% chance of a 25% loss   Yes *(2)*   No *(0)*

   c) had a 90% chance of a 25% gain
      and a 10% chance of a 10% loss   Yes *(1)*   No *(0)*

3. In the handling of your finances, would you be willing to take above-average risks in order to seek greater growth with some or all of your investable funds?

                                       Yes *(2)*   No *(0)*

If yes, indicate what percent of your investable funds you would be willing to place in investments of above-average risk.

                                       _____ percent

> *11% and above = 2; 10% and below = 0*

4. Choose five items you consider more important than the two remaining items. Then rank the items in order of importance. Write 5 before the most important, 4 before the next most important, then 3, then 2, and then 1.

    a) ____ Liquidity (availability)
    b) ____ Current Income from Investments
    c) ____ Future Income
    d) ____ Inflation Protection (assuring purchasing power)
    e) ____ Income Tax Deferral/Relief
    f) ____ Capital Growth
    g) ____ Safety of Principal

> *3 points if most important is c, d, e, or f;*
> *0 points if most important is a, b, or g.*

Evaluation of Results

Total Potential Score: 23 points

Score	Risk Type
0–5	No risk-taking ability
6–10	Minimizing risk is of maximum importance
11–15	Have ability to invest in all investments, but high-risk-type investments must be kept to 10–15% of total investments
16–20	Any percentage in high risk
21–23	One-way ticket to Las Vegas

Question 4: If a, b, or g is rated 5 (top priority) then the overall rating might be on the high side.

appendices

We also develop a weighted average for couples on their "major" concerns.

Example

Mary		Robert		Weighted Average
Current Income	5	Capital Growth	8	Inflation Protection
Inflation Protection	4	Inflation Protection		
Tax Control	3	Future Income	5	Current Income
Future Income	2	Tax Control	5	Capital Growth
Safety of Principal	1	Liquidity	5	Tax Control
			5	Future Income

Selected Bibliography

Bortz, Walter M. II, M.D. *Dare to Be 100.* Fireside, 1996.

Chopra, Deepak. *Ageless Body, Timeless Mind: The Quantum Alternative to Growing Old.* Three Rivers Press, 1998

Clason, George S. *The Richest Man in Babylon.* New American Library, 1988.
> There still may be hardbound and cassette versions of this book available, but the reissued version by New American Library is the least expensive choice for what might be one of the best investments you have ever made.

Cooper, M.D., Kenneth. *The New Aerobics.* Bantam Books, 1970.

Dychtwald, Ken. *Age Wave: How the Most Important Trend of Our Time Will Change Our Future.* Bantam Doubleday Dell Publishers, 1990.

James, William. *The Will to Believe and Other Essays in Popular Philosophy* and *Human Immortality* (in one volume). Dover Publications, 1985.

Martin, Clement G., M.D. *How to Live to Be 100, Actively, Healthily, Vigorously.* Frederick Fell, Inc., 1963.

Perls, Thomas T., M.D., and Dr. Margery Hutter Silver. *Living to 100: Lessons in Living to Your Maximum Potential at Any Age.* Basic Books, 2000.

Roszkowski, Michael J. "Personal Financial Risk Tolerance." The American College, Bryn Mawr, Pennsylvania, 1992.

Schwartz, Joseph *Don't Ever Retire But Do It Early and Often*. Farnsworth Publishing Company, 1979.

Stransky, Fred W. *The Good News About Nutrition, Exercise, and Weight Control*. Oakland University Press, 2001.

About the Author

Donald Ray Haas, CLU, ChFC, CFP, MSFS, is the president of Haas Financial Services, a registered investment advisor, and the president and registered principal of Haas Financial Products, a securities broker-dealer.

He is the author of *Money Monitor,* a monthly client newsletter, and of the book *Financial Planning for the Baby Boomer Client.* In 2001 he received the Loren Dunton Memorial Award, given by the National Association of Insurance and Financial Advisors for significant contributions to the financial advising profession and the public.

In 2002 Haas was selected for the Michigan Insurance Hall of Fame and he was recently listed as one of the 300 best financial advisors in America in Worth magazine. He is a past member of the board of directors of the Society of Financial Service Professionals and served as president of its Detroit chapter. He is a twenty-eight-year member of the Million Dollar Round Table and a thirty-three-year recipient of the National Quality Award.

Haas lectures frequently on financial planning to groups of professionals throughout the world. He has been an adjunct instructor in financial planning at Lawrence Technological

University and has served on the Board of Practice Standards of the Certified Financial Planner Board of Standards.

After receiving his undergraduate degree from the University of Michigan and a master's degree in education from Wayne State University, Haas joined the trumpet section of the Detroit Symphony Orchestra, a position he held for twenty years. During most of those years, he developed his financial planning career, and since retiring from the DSO in 1973, has devoted his full time to financial planning.